YEAR-ROUND EDUCATION

Year-Round Education

Its Problems and Prospects from Kindergarten to College

By

Clarence A. Schoenfeld

Associate Professor of Journalism and

Associate Director of the Summer Sessions

The University of Wisconsin

And

Neil Schmitz

Department of English

Stanford University

With a Foreword by John R. Little, Dean of the Summer Session, The University of Colorado

DEMBAR EDUCATIONAL
RESEARCH SERVICES, INC.
MADISON 1, INC.

YEAR-ROUND EDUCATION

Printed in the United States of America. First Edition.
Library of Congress Catalog Card Number 64–14824

It is necessary for all concerned to have an unswerving commitment to improvement. Each and every one of us should give first priority to a commitment to the modernization of the particular facet of education for which he is responsible . . . . The summer program has tremendous possibilities to serve an even wider and deeper clientele than it has in the past, as a catalytic agent, daring to present, establish, and maintain new arrangements—for students on the one hand and for faculty on the other—which, upon observation, will be adapted and adopted for the rest of the year.—John Guy Fowlkes.

TABLE OF CONTENTS

Foreword	ix
Preface	xxvii
By Way of Introduction	1
The All-Year Elementary and Secondary School	9
The Year-Round College and University	39
Problems and Prospects	87
References	103

Foreword[*]

THE TYPICAL large American university has for many years operated an extensive program of instruction, research, and related services on a year-round basis. Many American colleges, especially those with sizeable teacher-training programs, have also maintained year-round instructional programs on a reasonably large scale. However, instructional facilities, if reasonably adequate for fall enrollments, are not being fully used in winter and spring and are often grossly underused in summer. Currently, colleges and universities enroll well over 4½ million students in the fall. By spring the enrollment has dwindled to less than 4 million and in summer it is no more than 1 million.

Recent modest increases and the projected immense impending "rising tide" of enrollment, together with greatly increasing educational costs, have caused legislatures, boards of control, and the people generally to examine more critically than ever before many aspects of educational efficiency. Chief among items coming under close scrutiny is the provision of educational opportunities and the degree of maximal full-scale instructional use of facilities and faculties, not only as reflected in the fall, but in all other terms as well.

Pressures from various constituencies have mounted to such an extent that legislatures, boards, and occasionally administrators, impatient with traditional deliberative faculty participation and concurrence in this type of educational policy decision, have mandated some rather abrupt calendar organizational changes. These changes have been brought into

* Summary of an address by Dean John R. Little to the North Central Conference on Summer Schools, Chicago, Illinois, March 17, 1963.

full effect too soon, before the need was great enough to insure success, and have created immense problems in implementation, particularly as related to faculty morale, work-load and compensation, purported loss of faculty research time in universities, increased instructional costs, increased service type costs, such as student services, registration, building maintenance, etc., the compressing of courses, the increasing of student loads, certain course-credit and student attendance problems, and conflicts with cultural mores exemplified in vacation and school attendance habits of the American people. In general, the studies upon which these decisions have been made, although numerous, have not been as complete as they might have been. There are some considerations important to faculty members, and other items important to students and their parents, which have not been fully explored.

STUDY OF 116 LARGE UNIVERSITIES

In a 1963 study of calendar patterns and plans in 116 of the largest American universities, it was found that eighty-nine or 77 percent are on the semester-summer session plan, including two which converted recently from the quarter. Twenty-two or 19 percent are on the quarter-summer session plan including five which converted recently to the quarter, and one which is moving to the four quarter plan. Five, or 4 percent, are on the trimester plan. Four of these (all Florida) operate the split-third term and Pittsburgh has a separate mid-summer session concurrent with the third term. Two-thirds (68) run summer terms of 10 or more weeks in length, typically of split-term type but frequently with an unbroken term of 10 weeks or longer.

About half reported that no studies were in progress and that no basic calendar changes were contemplated. Nineteen universities have completed studies, made changes and contemplate no further studies or changes. Nine are considering the trimester with or without the split-third term, two are considering the 4-quarter plan, one is considering an earlier start in the fall, six are thinking of lengthening the summer session, and several are thinking of administratively integrating the summer session. One-third are conducting studies with three general possibilities under consideration:

1. Continuing (or changing to) the semester-summer session plan but with the possibility of lengthening, expanding and otherwise strengthening summer instructional programs as enrollment pressures increase,
2. Continuing (or changing to) the 10 or 11-week quarter-summer session plan with or without a separate summer session and with the possibility of adding a full summer quarter when actually needed.
3. Changing to the trimester (three short semesters) plan with or without a summer session.

It appears that while there is widespread great concern among institutions of higher learning in this country about improving year-round aspects, there are many (half or more) who apparently feel they are doing as well as they can under present circumstances and, although interested in developing their year-round programs as much as possible, are not greatly motivated toward making major changes until the need is greater than at present.[1]

THE SEMESTER PLAN

Contrary to previous reports indicating 15 weeks as a semester[2], the typical American college and university semester is 17 weeks exclusive of orientation, advising, registration and commencement. The semester-summer session year typically consists of two such semesters with a summer-semester or session of from 8 to 12 weeks, sometimes split and often supplemented by a concurrent and mid-summer term of 6 or 8

---

1 The above information is fully corroborated by a similar study in 1963 of the 107 colleges and universities holding membership in the North Central Conference on Summer Schools.

2 *Report of the Committee on The University Calendar of the American Association of Collegiate Registrars and Admissions*, 1961, page 8.

weeks. Classes for the fall semester normally begin the third week of September and continue through January; the spring semester runs from February through the first week in June with summer sessions of 8 to 12 weeks beginning about mid-June ending at various times up to the end of August. The major vacations, other than one-day holidays, break into the semesters with the Christmas vacation in late December through the first few days of January, leaving a detached period of 2 weeks or more in January, and spring vacation taking typically one week in March or April. Final examinations are usually given during the last 6 to 10 days of the semester. Credits are computed on the semester-hour basis with the typical semester class hour of fifty minutes. However, in most summer sessions the class hour is extended to sixty minutes with the seventy-five or ninety-minute period becoming increasingly popular as a means of providing equivalent class-time per credit hour. Summer programs in institutions under the semester plan are with very few exceptions administered under a separate dean or director. The recent change at the University of Michigan is an exception.

Under the semester plan, normally carrying one semester hour per week of attendance (17 hours), it is possible for an accelerating student to complete the baccalaureate degree in six semesters and two summer sessions, attending classes for 122 weeks earning 122+ semester credits. Acceleration beyond this is possible for superior students who are capable of carrying more than 17 semester credits per semester and who have the sustained motivation and energy to accomplish this objective.

Among main advantages, which faculties using the semester are very reluctant to change or lose, are the 17-week length of prime-attendance time, allowing for larger units (courses) of instruction, more student time for independent study, laboratory work, reading, writing, deliberation and maturity, and providing more faculty time for the instruction and evaluation of students, and for reading, writing, re-doing courses, and research. Also, the semester beginnings and endings coincide with schools and other colleges, providing easy entry and re-entry, and matching the attendance and vacation habits of the American people. The semester plan provides a full 9 months of prime-attendance time with maximum enrollment possible throughout the entire period.

Principal disadvantages are the lack of vacation and term flexibility present in other plans, the presence of the detached "lame-duck" period after Christmas, and the inability to divide the total year into equal parts, resulting in summer terms of shorter lengths which have come to be different in status, types of program, clientele, faculty salaries, perhaps program depth and quality, and in other respects.

THE QUARTER OR FOUR-TERM PLAN

Typically the quarter plan consists of a 9-month academic year divided into three 11-week terms exclusive of orientation, advising, registration and commencement, with either an undivided or divided summer quarter (5½—5½ weeks) or a 6, 8, 9, 10 or 11-week summer session, sometimes supplemented by a mid-summer 6 or 8 week concurrent term. There are a few institutions using four 10-week terms. The 8 and 10-week summer sessions are sometimes divided also, and, in addition, there may be one or more pre or post sessions or other special purpose terms. The summer quarter or session is typically administered under a separate dean or director but in some of the recent conversions is brought under the school and college deans.

The quarters are scheduled to provide an unbroken 11-week period for classes except for Thanksgiving holidays and national or special school holidays. Fall quarter classes begin with the third or fourth week of September and sometimes as late as the first week of October, ending in the second or third week of December. Two or three-week Christmas vacations are possible. Ten or 11-week winter and spring quarters are scheduled, with an intervening spring vacation of one week, and ending in the first or second week of June. There is more time pressure between January and June than in the fall, however, and many winter and spring quarters can only provide 10 or 10½ weeks for classes rather than 11. The examination period is usually the last 6 days of the term.

Credit hours are computed in quarter hours although some recently converted schools continued with the semester hour unit, increasing proportionately the class time (more class sessions per week and/or up to 75 minute periods) and reducing proportionately the number of hours attempted. By using the larger semester-credit unit students may take fewer courses and hours to get equivalent total loads and credit in the 9-month academic year. It is possible for a student carrying a normal load (10 to 12 semester hours or 16 quarter hours) to attend for any combination of quarters or summer terms totaling 9 to 11 weeks with maximum acceleration under normal course load conditions, making the baccalaureate degree possible in eleven successive quarters (121 weeks with 120 or more semester hours). Acceleration for superior students capable of carrying the equivalent of 18 or more semester hours per term could make possible the completion of the baccalaureate degree in 10 quarters or 2½ calendar years.

Principal advantages are the flexibility of term and vacation time for both students and faculty. This flexibility also gives wider options in course selection and in changing sequences and adjusting major-minor patterns. No quarter is interrupted for more than national or local holidays except at Thanksgiving time. The term beginnings and endings coincide with other colleges and the schools, providing for easy entry and reentry, and also are not in conflict with established attendance and vacation habits of the American people. This plan most readily accommodates the required student-teaching for those preparing to teach. The quarter plan using the semester hour unit provides for more concentrated study in fewer subjects and the three or four terms can be of equal length. A fourth term or quarter may be added when needed without disruption of any phase or portion of the institution's program. The quarter also provides a full 9 months of prime-attendance time with maximum enrollment possible throughout the entire period.

Main disadvantages are that the quarter or 10-week term is somewhat short for best academic use as the basic time unit, necessitating smaller instructional units (courses), and not providing as much time for deliberating, reading, writing, laboratory work, student maturing, and time for the increasing reliance now placed on independent study. Faculty time for teaching, examining grading, etc., is shorter when considered on a single course basis; however, it is the same for both students and faculty when considered on an academic year basis. More time is required in registration and in final examinations, although this would not be true if a split-third term or summer semester is added in the trimester or semester plans.

THE TRIMESTER PLAN

The trimester, defined by Webster as one of three terms into which the academic year is divided at some educational institutions[3], is actually a short semester. Typically it is 15 weeks in length, exclusive of orientation, advising, registration and commencement as compared with the typical 17-week semester. Under the trimester plan three 15-week terms constitute the academic year with the separate summer session eliminated or running concurrently to the third trimester in mid-summer as at Pittsburgh (6-weeks). A small number of institutions use a split-third term with half-terms of 7½ weeks each, the second serving in place of the traditional summer session to provide flexibility and accommodate the needs of special groups such as elementary and secondary teachers.

The first trimester begins in late August or early September and ends before Christmas, the second running from New Year's to mid-April and the third extending from the end of April to early August with approximately four weeks set aside for vacations and housekeeping[4]. Examinations usually occupy

3 *Webster's Third New International Dictionary* (unabridged), G. C. Mirriam Co., 1961, page 2445.

4 These dates of course may vary from campus to campus.

the last six days of the term. The vacation periods except for Thanksgiving, national, or special local holidays are scheduled outside the term, thus providing an uninterrupted 15-week period for class purposes including examinations, except in the split-third term when a short interim between half-terms is planned.

Class credit hours are computed in semester hours with a similar number of clock hours of class work per credit-hour as provided by institutions on the semester plan. Under the trimester plan, the full year is 45 weeks as compared with 42, 44, 45, 46 or 48 weeks, depending on the length of summer terms, under the quarter or semester plans. On the basis of one semester-hour of credit work per week of attendance, the normal student load would be 15 semester hours per term, making it possible to complete a baccalaureate degree program in eight trimesters (120 weeks and 120 semester hours).

There is no specific pattern for faculty teaching schedules and loads. At Pittsburgh the faculty normally are employed on a two-term basis with the option of teaching the third term for an increase of 33⅓ percent in pay. The teaching load at Pittsburgh now averages 7.6 semester hours per term as against 12.2 before the changeover. This reduction has been accomplished mainly by extensive use of large lecture classes supplemented by discussion sections with teaching associates.[5] At the Florida universities, 2½ term faculty appointments are used with a salary increase of 11 percent for the additional time required. No additional faculty have been employed for the trimester operation and the per term teaching load remains essentially the same as before in Florida[6]. In each of the above, it is expected that eventually leave time will be equivalent to at least one trimester out of six. Some faculty have taught straight through eleven trimesters without

---

5 Information from personal conversations with administrative officers at the University of Pittsburgh, February, 1963.

6 Information from personal conversations with administrative officers at The University of Florida, Gainesville, and Florida State University, Tallahassee, February, 1963.

interruption since 1959 at Pittsburgh. At Harpur College it is expected faculty work plans will embrace a 6-term cycle within which a professor will teach four terms with no more than three teaching terms falling consecutively[7].

Although the 1963 surveys of large universities (and also colleges and universities of the North Central Conference) do not reflect it, it was reported by Stickler that "at present some 30 institutions either operate on the trimester calendar or have made the basic decision to shift to this type of year-round operation within the foreseeable future[8]. Sidney Tickton's booklet on year-round education, lists fourteen (6 universities and 8 colleges) which have actually gone to the trimester or are in process of changeover[9]. However, the University of Michigan, one of those listed, has not and may not change from semester to trimester plan.

Principal advantages of the trimester plan are that a major portion of the academic values of the semester (time necessary for quality education, etc.) are present and also most of the flexibility qualities such as term and vacation, course selection, change of major, etc., of the quarter plan. It is claimed by some that a full semester's work can and is being done by both students and faculty in the 15-week trimester. It has the advantage of equal-length terms and this would assist toward equalizing status, character of offerings, and faculty leave plans and pay. The trimester, operating 45 weeks per year, is said to make it possible for the university to educate more people with little additional plant and equipment. It is said to provide more flexibility for faculty in planning research and gives greater opportunity for students to accelerate. Library usage by students and studying generally is sharply up in schools

---

7 *PMLA*, "For Members Only," March, 1963, page iv.

8 Stickler, W. Hugh, *The Year-Round Academic Calendar,* an address given to the Conference of Academic Deans of Southern States, Dallas, Texas, November 17, 1962.

9 Tickton, Sidney G., *The Year-Round Campus Catches On,* The Fund For the Advancement of Education, New York, January, 1963.

using the trimester with time spent on activities dropping significantly.

The main disadvantages are that the trimester under present conditions has not met enrollment expectations and that institutions on this plan are in the extremely uncomfortable position of being out-of-step with the schools and with other colleges and universities, and with the attendance and vacation habits of the American people. By reducing easy entry and reentry opportunities, enrollments have undoubtedly been affected adversely. (At Pittsburgh enrollments are down significantly.) Many Florida students[10] complained that the courses were considerably compressed and that they were consistently hurried, particularly at examination time. Average student credit loads apparently do not remain at semester level but are adjusted downward through student initiative. Upper division and graduate students at Pittsburgh complained that needed courses were not offered in summer. Faculty members on the trimester complained of a loss of research time, disproportionate pay for added work, and reported that students will usually do 15 weeks' work, not 17 weeks' work, in 15 weeks. (It should be noted that some of these problems are functional and will undoubtedly be relieved as experience is gained and adjustments made.)

CURRENT DEVELOPMENTS

Although plans for the three-semester (15–15–7½, 7½) year had been approved at the University of Michigan, neither the funds nor the students necessary to fully implement the 3rd full semester appeared to be at hand for the 1963–64 year. As a result, Michigan will continue on a semester plan in 1963–64 with fall and spring semesters of 16 weeks each (shortened from 17) and a summer semester of 8 weeks, and with no change in faculty pay plans. In the fall, classes will begin on Tuesday after Labor Day, with orientation and regis-

10 Information gained through interviews with students and faculty at The University of Florida, Gainesville, Florida State University, Tallahassee, and The University of Pittsburgh, February, 1963.

tration having taken place before, and end after 16 weeks on December 21, thus eliminating the "lame-duck" period. Three weeks will be allowed for vacation (the normal 2 weeks at Christmas combined with the 1-week between-semester break) with classes starting on January 16, and with orientation and registration having been completed. There will be one week of vacation in March and classes will end on May 16. Commencement will be on May 23, allowing a period for exam grading and cleanup, faculty meetings for approving of degrees, Regents' meetings, etc. It is planned that when need is fully demonstrated by enrollment increases, and when the money is available, the summer semester will be lengthened and the course offerings expanded.

The University of Illinois and the University of California also are considering calendar changes.

PURPORTED DIFFERENCES BETWEEN "THE YEAR" AND SUMMER SESSION

The criticism has been leveled that summer sessions are different in status in the eyes of the general public, the faculty and students; different in salaries paid the faculty; different in character and quality of program; and different in length of terms. It has been said that only by eliminating all of these primary differences can true equality be attained and year-round programs be achieved, in fact.

The statement is largely true but not in its entirety. In my opinion, I would add that an institution to achieve maximal year-round service must also have large numbers of additional students willing to attend in summer, and some who would be willing to absent themselves in fall. In addition, the money to meet the additional costs involved must be available. There are many institutions which have been aware of these differences and have been laboring, with at least modest success, toward minimizing them. There are significant numbers on both quarter and semester plans where the remaining differences are few.

Salaries are improving rapidly in summer with a sizeable number of summer salary scales now at par. However, in my opinion, salary differentials of this type are indefensible as a policy matter and should certainly be eliminated at the earliest possible time. This constitutes one of the principal cost differentials which has been making it possible for some summer sessions to be self-supporting. The faculty has been and is being exploited in proportion to existing salary differentials. Such differentials not only exist in many summer sessions, but also in all of the five universities where the trimester is now operating. Tuitions and student fees must also be brought to parity, both with respect to over-all rates, and in state institutions, to state residency and nonresidency status. It is not sound policy, nor fair, to charge proportionately more in summer than fall or spring, nor is it right for the resident students of the state, or the state itself, to subsidize the education of those from other states more in summer than is done in fall or spring.

Character and quality, reflected in level and quality of students, number, variety and quality of courses, quality of teaching, quality of research, and general intellectual-cultural atmosphere are now equal in some institutions and in a few are actually superior to that in the fall and winter or spring. Much remains to be done, however, in bringing up the general level in the United States.

Insofar as length of term is concerned, it is my belief that, all other factors being equal, it would be desirable from an administrative standpoint but not essential that terms be exactly equal in length. It should be noted that those who belabor this point are willing to sacrifice it in establishing the split-third term or concurrent short summer session. Experiments and research[11] have demonstrated that under good con-

---

11 Kanan and Ziebarth, *Comparisons of Student Achievements in Summer With Second Quarter,* Bureau of Institutional Research, University of Minnesota, 1961.

ditions, most college level courses can successfully be taught with equal or near equal student achievement in summer terms. No significant differences were found in student achievement between the 11-week quarter and the 5-week summer term at The University of Minnesota.

"TOOLING UP" TO EDUCATE MORE STUDENTS

Most would agree that, in degrees varying from very small to very large, many institutions operate year-round programs. The fact remains, however, that as indicated previously, American colleges and universities, crowded by 4½ million students last fall, are about on a comfortable basis this winter and spring with 4 million or less, and next summer we will be grossly under-enrolled with about 1 million students in the 1400 institutions attempting summer instructional programs[12]. Many student-stations will be unused for many, many hours in summer, while at the same time many universities will be turning away qualified applicants for the coming fall. Enrollments are obviously badly peaked in fall, perhaps about right in winter, light in spring and very light in summer. However, until pressures are great enough to force students into these unused spaces, summer enrollments, regardless of calendar, will not increase spectacularly. Under 1962–63 conditions light summer use is not so bad, but thinking forward to 1965 and 1970, we would indeed be remiss if we did not attempt by every legitimate, educationally sound means to "tool up" toward increasing the numbers we can educate and without increasing instructional facilities proportionately. This can only be done through increased summer and spring attendance, primarily by an institution's own degree-seeking students. Toward

12 Assuming that enrollments are at capacity in the fall, this means that there will exist in 1963 over 3 million student-semesters of student-quarters of learning space (30 million potential SCH) and time.

accomplishing these ends it is suggested that institutions might consider the following possibilities:

1. Establish educational policies and programs in order to make it possible
   (a) for qualified freshmen and transfer students to enter at the beginning of any term and work toward their educational objectives, and
   (b) for former students to continue progress toward and complete degree programs in any term;
2. Use all legitimate means, such as news stories, leaflets, announcements, press releases, discussions, conferences, etc., and in addition, academic advising and counseling programs and other internal devices could be used far more effectively, and vigorously than in the past to inform and encourage the school's own degree students to attend in spring and summer, and encouragement should be given to qualified non-degree summer-only students having substantial educational goals to attend also;
3. Encourage the year-round attendance of larger numbers of qualified students whose homes are in the area but who need to work while attending on a part-time basis, particularly in summer;
4. Develop a plan whereby institutions as a group in a given year (perhaps 1968) might agree to cooperate in establishing a plan for limiting fall enrollments. If an institution plans to admit 3000 freshmen in a given year, a major portion (perhaps 2/3) of the qualified applicants could be admitted to fall term on a scholastic qualifications or first come basis, others could be deferred to summer and spring. The same general plan with different quotas could also be used for transfer admissions. If a large number of institutions, perhaps all in a state or an area, agreed to such a plan and announced it two years in advance of its application, it could be made to work;

5. Offer incentives such as an abundance of scholarships or reduced tuition rates for summer for those attending three terms in succession, including summer;
6. Control course sequences so that certain key courses would be available during only one or two terms per year and one of these should be summer;
7. Allow beginning students at least two terms to prove themselves before suspension rules apply. Those beginning in summer could be extended through spring, others for two terms only;
8. Curtail the building of additional duplicated classroom and teaching laboratory facilities, refusing to admit new students or continue those not doing well, beyond certain modest growth limits, until certain predetermined attendance goals are reached in summer (perhaps 60, 70 or 80 percent of fall enrollment);
9. Encourage and perhaps require students entering in the fall to attend for three consecutive terms, then "lay off" the next fall term;
10. Cooperate closely through inter-institutional committees, perhaps including states, areas, and associations working with the public through newspapers and other media toward needed changes in the cultural patterns, mainly the school attendance and vacation habits, to aid in levelling the fall peak and raising the summer valley on our attendance graphs.

It is my opinion when institutions actually recognize the need and make extensive, local, state, regional, and national plans for such year-round programs and begin to phase them in, demonstrating a willingness to change existing patterns and also that the enrollment is actually increasing in spring and summer, the additional needed funds will be forthcoming.

ACCELERATION VS. TIME FOR MATURITY

Although there is no appreciable difference in acceleration opportunity between the three plans, much has been said about acceleration as one of the chief reasons for emphasis on year-round programs, particularly by those advocating the trimester. In my opinion, acceleration should be a secondary reason, one not to be strongly emphasized. True, the opportunity should be provided for acceleration toward the attainment of a degree in minimum time, and also opportunity to attend on a part-time basis around the calendar; however, I find strong resistance to the idea of straight-through, year-round full-load attendance. Students almost unanimously favor a plan providing opportunity for year-round study and acceleration but a large majority do not participate nor plan to participate to any degree in acceleration. "It's fine for someone else but not for me," is a typical attitude.

I have found that after a semester or two under trimester pressure, students tend to drop a course or two and at next registration enroll for a slightly lighter load. They make their own adjustments and tend to defeat the goal of large scale acceleration. Their average credit-loads were reduced in Florida by almost 1 credit-hour per student after the changeover, with the average student load being reduced to slightly over 14 semester hours. At Pittsburgh, not many were accelerating toward degrees in less than 4 years and these were mainly studying in the professions, not in the so-called academic disciplines. However, these students were highly motivated and were very grateful for the opportunity to attend year-round in order to get on a job sooner. The average student credit hour load at Pittsburgh was about 11 semester hours in fall and winter and 7.5 in the third term. Acceleration as well as summer enrollments have been disappointing at Pittsburgh.

In my opinon, acceleration for undergraduates should be mainly for the excellent and superior students. There are substantial numbers of these who are fully capable and should be encouraged to proceed at a rapid rate and who will be bored, if denied. Many graduate and upper division students can profit by acceleration, however. Time for maturity is more important for freshmen and lower division students and I doubt that many should accelerate merely for the sake of getting through faster. Rather, they should be encouraged to take additional electives in which they have interest, to broaden and improve their education. The required 120 semester hours should be considered only as a minimum and certainly could not be considered typical, nor indicative of a good education. Acceleration should be mainly for established graduate and upper division students, superior students at any level, and mature students who are highly motivated to finish degree programs and get jobs. It should be established as a principle that in a calendar year, full-time students taking normal loads under any calendar system should be expected to complete about 1 semester hour per week attended. Good students should do more, weaker students and those with substantial outside work or activities should do proportionately less, as determined in consultation with faculty advisors.

WHICH CALENDAR PLAN?

I find it logical to conclude that colleges and universities can effectively prepare themselves to approach their own maximal year-round potential, which will not be identical with that of any other institution, under any one of the three basic plans, the quarter, the trimester, or the semester. Certainly there is no one plan which clearly outranks all others in total merit. Each has its strengths and weaknesses. All institutions are concerned. Many have studied but very few have made major basic calendar changes. Many are continuing their own basic plan with a general lengthening and strengthening of the third term or summer semester. I believe that although it is shorter, those on the semester plan should call their summer program a summer semester from now on. All should work as rapidly as possible toward reducing the differences in term lengths, although they do not need to be identical to be successful, and toward eliminating such differences as exist in faculty salaries, quality and depth of program, teaching and grading standards, etc., and as a result the status differential, where it exists, will gradually disappear.

If an institution has had satisfactory experience with the current plan and is relatively happy with it, I would ask, why change? It is possible, feasible, no more costly and much less disruptive to adapt an existing plan, than to make a major changeover. The recent experience of those who have made a major basic changeover of calendar indicates that changes should be made on an evolutionary basis rather than abruptly. The institution should be concerned with year-round operation of facilities (the university, not individuals; no one should teach more than 2½ terms per year); remuneration should not be reduced nor conditions of employment worsened for faculty; a less time-consuming system of registration should be devised, and decisions for change and plans should be made well in advance with full faculty participation and concurrence, and should be effected only after the need arises through enrollment pressures, and after the additional necessary funds become available.

Preface

CAUGHT between vastly increasing student needs and relatively decreasing school resources—professional educators, concerned parents, and politicians are talking today about many means of adjusting supply to demand at all levels of education, from kindergarten to college. Among the favorite devices in this current American dialogue is the year-round calendar.

What are the facts about the all-year school? Has it ever worked? Does it produce measurable economies? Does it really offer acceleration and enrichment? Can students and staff stand the pace? Do social gains outweigh any administrative headaches? Is the public ready? What are the principles that must guide calendar planning? In short, is year-round education panacea or pitfall?

YEAR-ROUND EDUCATION—Problems and Prospects tries to answer these questions in practical terms. In this attempted analysis of the all-year school, the authors review the long history of academic-calendar juggling, look at recent experiments, and bring to bear on the matter a fair range of research data from the fields of psychology, meteorology, physiology, sociology, commerce, and education. What emerges is an assessment of a national issue that tries to focus our attention on demonstrable facts rather than on popular fancy. Chapters deal with the all-year elementary and secondary school, the year-round university, and the prospects for both. In all of these discussions, "education" is equated with preparatory, undergraduate, and graduate instruction in conventional settings, leaving to another study the equally important questions about year-round technical, vocational, and adult education on campus and off.

The senior author is the author of *The University and Its Publics, Effective Feature Writing, and Publicity Media and Methods.* The junior author is the former editor of *The New Idea.* It is perhaps not surprising, therefore, that they conclude the subject at hand is one which has "special ability to attract to American education the public interest which is the prerequisite for essential public understanding and support" in the continuing evolution of American education for American society.

Like any research report, this monograph is as much the product of a team as of the ostensible authors. Included among those who have lent invaluable insight or inspiration are:

Dr. Robert DeZonia, the Joint Staff of the Wisconsin Coordinating Committee on Higher Education; Profs. Clifford Liddle, Alden White, Philip Lambert, Theodore Harris, George Field, Robert Hughes, and L. Joseph Lins, The University of Wisconsin; Deans F. Chandler Young, Bruce Davidson, and Wilson Thiede, The University of Wisconsin; Dr. Russell Lewis, the Wisconsin State Department of Public Instruction; Dr. Oluf Davidson, the American College Testing Program; Deans Robert Norris and Adolph Suppan, The University of Wisconsin-Milwaukee; Allan Ostar, the Association of Land Grant Colleges and State Universities; Dr. Edd Miller, the University of Michigan; Dean Royden Dangerfield, the University of Illinois; Dean Frank Burrin, Purdue University; Dean Robert Rickey, Indiana University; Dean John R. Little, the University of Colorado; Dean E. W. Ziebarth, the University of Minnesota; Dr. Harold Haswell, U.S. Office of Education; Dr. John Schmid, the University of Arkansas; Arnold Caucutt, Dembar Educational Research Services; and Mrs. Phyl Murphy and Barbara Sanderson, The University of Wisconsin staff.

Because of the appearance of the excellent *Year-Round Operation in American Universities*, a committee report to the

Association of University Summer Session Deans and Directors, this monograph does not go into detail on the outlines and assessments of various third-term patterns covered in that study, issued at Boulder, Colorado, in October, 1963.

Monograph royalties are assigned to the Dean Lindley J. Stiles/School of Education *Wisconsin Trophy for Teaching Fund* through The University of Wisconsin Foundation.

Our particular thanks go to Dr. L. H. Adolfson, Dean of Extension and Director of the Summer Sessions, The University of Wisconsin, for his encouragement and counsel.

November 15, 1963 C.A.S.
Madison, Wisconsin N.S.

YEAR-ROUND EDUCATION

Problems and Prospects

I

By Way of Introduction

BARRING LOVE and war, few enterprises are undertaken with such abandon, by such a diversity of amateur and professional practitioners, with so paradoxical a mixture of political appetite and philosophical altruism, as the great American pastime of Educational Planning.

By common consent, more education for more people is a good thing. But wherein lies the goodness, and what can be done to ensure its efficient pursuit? On these questions there is confusion of counsel, and only the most uncritical minds are free from doubt.

Nowhere in recent months has the confusion been more consistent than in the burgeoning discussion of year-round schooling, at all levels of education from kindergarten to college.

NATIONAL HEADLINES

Typical of the turmoil on the subject of the year-round college is this fall of 1963 story by Associated Press reporters G. K. Hodenfield and Murray Chass:

> The leisurely academic life at college is going the way of the raccoon coat, the Charleston, and bathtub gin.
>
> It is harder to get into college, and harder to stay there, than it was a generation ago. There is more to learn, more who want to learn it, and no place for the laggard.
>
> In an effort to cope with the swelling hordes of high school graduates seeking a higher education, many colleges and universities are turning to various forms of a year-around program.
>
> One which seems to be catching on generally is the trimester, sometimes referred to as the "trimonster."

By any name it is a speed-up, and when it comes in, something wonderful—the art of learning leisurely—goes out of college.

Instead of the traditional two semesters of 16–18 weeks, with a long summer vacation, the trimester plan has three terms of 14–15 weeks, with a one-month break in late summer.

A student attending eight consecutive trimesters can graduate in two years and eight months, instead of the usual three years and nine months. Many students, particularly those working their way through school, attend only two trimesters a year and graduate in the traditional time.

The advantages of the trimester are obvious, and difficult to debate:

A college on the trimester plan can accommodate 30 per cent or more students with no more classrooms and with only a modest increase in staff. With college enrolments jumping from four million now to eight million in 1970, this program may be the only salvation for hard-pressed state institutions.

Students can cut years off the time they normally would spend preparing themselves for a career. This particularly is true of the growing number who go on to professional or graduate school.

The traditional long summer vacation is a throw-back to the day when young people were needed at home on the farm in summer, and that day has long since passed.

The keynote of the trimester is efficiency. And there, perhaps, is its greatest drawback.

There is limited space on the educational assembly line for mind-sharpening bull sessions, for browsing in the library and reading for pleasure, for meditation, and absorbing that which is being learned, for attending plays and concerts, and for just plain riverbank cogitation on the state of the world and its complex problems.

Says Ross R. Ogelsby, Dean of Students at Florida State University:

"The trimester robs students of many things, but what they miss most of all is thinking time.' "

The University of Pittsburgh pioneered the trimester plan in September, 1959, and it is now an accepted way of academic life there. All four of Florida's state universities went on the program last fall, as did Jacksonville, Fla. University, a private institution.

The University of Michigan may join the trimester corps this September. The University of California, the world's largest institution of higher education, and Ohio State University are giving the three-term plan serious thought.

Pittsburgh Chancellor Edward H. Litchfield, father of the trimester, believes the plan will spread nationwide.

"We can predict with some confidence," he said recently, "that during this decade the traditional program will become an anchronism in higher education, and a rapidly declining characteristic of secondary schools systems as well."

Litchfield began thinking about a trimester program when he was a freshman at the University of Michigan in 1932.

"I went the year 'round by piecing together formal summer work," he said. "I was just interested in studying and working away. I didn't want to be sent home in May, not to come back until September. That wasn't my notion of how to get through."

When he arrived on the Pitt campus in 1956 he started talking up the trimester. Three years later it went into effect.

However, if it is true that national adoption of the trimester plan is as inevitable as death and taxes, it also is true that in some quarters it is just about as popular.

When the Florida Legislature forced the four state universities there to adopt the trimester last fall, there were howls of outrage.

Now, after a hectic, one-year trial, the howls have diminished to moans.

If the trimester survives in Florida, other state legislatures may demand something similar for their public institutions. This is the Florida pattern:

Work that had been covered in 16 weeks was compressed into 14. End-of-term examination periods were cut from two weeks to one. To make the actual time-in-class the same under the trimester as it was under the semester, each class period was lengthened by seven minutes.

Including examination periods, the trimesters ran from Sept. 10 to Dec. 22, Jan. 7 to April 12, and April 29 to Aug. 9. Christmas vacation, Easter vacation, and registration took up the time between trimesters.

To accommodate the thousands of teachers who return to the campus for summer school each year, the third trimester was divided into two equal parts. Regular students had the option of attending either, neither, or both halves. Teachers, still in their classrooms when the third trimester started, were in effect restricted to the second half, starting in mid-June.

The Florida universities had a 14-month period in which to prepare for the trimester. But when it came, few of the faculty and even fewer of the students were ready.

The transition was rough.

Freshmen found college work harder than they had ever imagined, and some foundered.

Upperclassmen found the speed-up forced them to reduce their academic loads. Working students had to ease their work schedules, and thus cut back their incomes.

Classroom lectures and textbook assignments designed for a 16-week semester had to be drastically revised for the 14-week trimester. One history professor solved his problem by dropping Formosa and Korea out of his course in Oriental history. An English professor said, "I'm just talking longer about fewer things."

These were the problems of transition, and all but a few die-hard opponents of the trimester acknowledged they would eventually be solved.

But cutting the academic term from 16 to 14 weeks has raised other problems for which there are no apparent solutions.

Professors of biology, chemistry, medicine, etc., say their students are denied time for important laboratory work. Music professors say their students have insufficient time to practice.

The time that faculty members can devote to independent study, travel, and research is sharply curtailed. This not only hampers the present faculty members, it makes it difficult for the universities to recruit top-notch teaching talent.

However, Chancellor Litchfield of Pittsburgh says of the trimester:

"The great advantage is that it keeps young, active minds working on academic subjects the larger part of the year instead of letting them do idle things. That use of human resources is important."

But critical professors in Florida say the trimester has meant sacrifices in the things which spell the differences between knowledge and wisdom, between book learning and true education.

Attendance at artists' performances, foreign film showings, concerts, and other cultural events has dropped sharply. The libraries report a great demand for reference works, little demand for leisure reading material. Volunteers to work on student publications are hard to find.

"The sad thing about it," a professor at the University of Florida said, "is that new generations of students will never know what they are missing."

LOCAL DEBATES

The year-round school topic is by no means merely the province of the wire services. It is increasingly coming into prominence in many local situations. Witness this recent story from the (Madison) *Wisconsin State Journal:*

Robert D. Gilberts, superintendent of schools, Wednesday told the Downtown Rotary club that the savings from year around use of schools may not be worth the problems it creates.

His speech to the Rotarians was an answer to George M. Jensen, Minneapolis, Minn., who last month told the club that the present eight-month school year "is as obsolete as an oxcart."

Gilberts admitted that the present school year may need some updating but said the quarter system as proposed by Jensen does not seem to be the answer.

He suggested instead that the school year be lengthened, not to save money or "just process one more carcass," but to "produce a better product."

Jensen, president of the Temtrol Corp., and former president of the Minneapolis board of education, is the organizing chairman of the National School Calendar Study Committee.

He has spoken on the long school year to Rotary clubs around the country, including the Downtown club here in June and the East Rotary on Tuesday.

Jensen proposes that the year be divided into quarters with each student going three quarters and vacationing one.

Under this plan, one-fourth of the pupils would be on vacation the year around and "a school built for 600 pupils could handle 800."

He said the quarter plan would be better for the students, the teachers, and make schools "less burdensome to taxpayers."

Gilberts said the 25 per cent saving on capital investment in school buildings "is diminished considerably" when spread over the 50-year life of a building.

He said capital investment and debt service comprise from zero to 20 per cent of schools' budgets. In Madison, the figure is about 14 per cent.

The most money that could be saved under the plan is 25 per cent of this figure. "But," he added, "the plan would result in higher administrative costs, transportation costs, and increased maintenance and operational costs."

He also pointed out other problems the quarter system would create:

One of these is that of vacations. The quarter system under which some students would have vacations in the winter, fall, or spring runs counter to the American tradition of summer vacation.

"We would have to change custom and this is not easy," he said.

Gilberts said he is not sure that all teachers would like working the year around, even if they received more pay. "Some feel that summers free to travel, study, or work are an important fringe benefit."

The system could also create real administrative problems regarding registration each quarter. Children would keep moving to new class groups and new teachers.

Seasonal activities like sports, drama, and forensics might also suffer. A boy on vacation during the fall quarter couldn't play football, and a girl on vacation in the spring might go to the spring formal.

The system would also create a transfer problem between schools, and eliminate the possibility of lengthening the school year if this should become necessary.

Gilberts said professional educators are not necessarily opposed to changing the school calendar. "Many have tried the quarter system, but not one has found enough in its favor to justify the change."

Gilberts said he favors lengthening the school year because it "provides all the advantages mentioned by Jensen except saving money."

"Only one-tenth of all taxes collected in the U. S. goes for public education," he said, but "education is the source most often put upon when it comes to saving money."

"Certainly we must be prudent and efficient in the operation of our schools, but we cannot solve all our tax problems in the area of education."

IN SEARCH OF FACTS

There is, at the outset, no real consensus as to the meaning of the term "year-round school" (or "all-year school"). Some use the term to describe an operation in which it is only the school physical plant that stays open for 12 months. To others the term implies continuous year-round work on the part of school staff and students. Between these two definitions there are about as many intergrades as there are proposals.

Objectives or advantages ascribed to year-round education are likewise varied. Politicians favoring the concept typically do so on grounds of economy, claiming substantial savings in buildings and instructional personnel. Those educators espousing year-round education prefer to speak of its value as a vehicle for academic acceleration, enrichment, or rehabilitation. Others see the scheme as solely an emergency measure which is required by a rush of students and which can as quickly be abandoned when "things get back to normal."

The voices of affirmation are equalled in their diversity and intensity only by the voices of dissent. We are told that year-round schooling is enormously expensive, that it will produce a generation of misfits, that no cadre of teachers can long sustain its debilitating pace, and that it runs counter to the socio-economic order, not to mention the North American climate.

Although it may seem to have burst over yesterday's horizon like a strange satellite, the idea of year-round education is not a product of the space age. In whole or in part its concepts and practices have been discussed and applied in various settings for many years. Consequently there is a substantial body of testimony and considerable research that can be cited, both for and against.

Such is the purpose of this monograph—to bring to bear on the subject of year-round education all the historical perspective and appropriate data the authors have been able to muster. What emerges is neither a defense nor a condemnation. If we have any theme it is this: that there may be times and places where year-round education is a worthwhile pattern, but it is no panacea. Like so many sweeping changes, it is as fraught with hazard as with promise. Its greatest utility may well lie in its special ability to attract to American education that indispensable public interest which is the prerequisite for essential public understanding and support.

II

The All-Year Elementary and Secondary School

THE CONCEPT of a school calendar wedded to the seasons of the year is an ancient Old World manifestation. The critical importance of "getting in the crops" had dictated for centuries that wars and education start in September and fade in spring. This pattern found ready acceptance in an agrarian America, and its persists today even though the summer for most people is less a harvest time than a vacation period.

Despite the pervasiveness of the nine-month school term, for at least 50 years some American educational planners have been describing, debating, and testing certain schedules that break away from the conventional academic calendar to provide instructional programs throughout the year. These patterns have varied in their objectives, their mechanisms, and their effectiveness.

Today, with American educators seemingly caught between the upper and nether millstones of vastly increasing student needs and relatively decreasing school resources, more and more professional and lay school men have turned to a consideration of the all-year elementary and secondary school as a possible means of adjusting supply to demand.

In this chapter, we define and describe the different forms the year-round school can take, we look briefly at the history of the movement, and we attempt an evaluation from several pertinent perspectives.

IN SEARCH OF A DEFINITION

The terms "all-year school" and "year-round school" have been used interchangeably to label a number of programs for the extension of the school year at the elementary and secondary levels. These patterns vary widely, and do not necessarily involve a full-year-round schedule for both students and faculty. For example, one program consistently described as an "all-year school" is simply an expansion of the conventional summer session and "involves no marked departure from present procedures."[1] Another plan places the teacher on a twelve-month basis of employment but leaves the student to his traditional 180-day class schedule. A 1954 Milwaukee (Wisconsin) Superintendency report, *The All-Year School,* attempted to delimit the definition of an all-year school: "The accepted definition . . . . is the four-quarter plan with schools operating regular classes throughout the year with one quarter of the pupils on vacation at all times."[2] Since, however, in nearly all the available literature on the subject, the four-quarter plan is considered as only one of several types of year-round schooling, the acceptance of this definition may be questioned. "It should be pointed out," another report declares, "that the term 'all-year school' is used in referring to a variety of arrangements which differ somewhat from one another".[3]

Perhaps the difficulty in evolving a precise meaning for the term, all-year school, may stem from its variance in motives. Some plans appear to be purely "economy minded," while other programs are particularly designed to accelerate the educational process. Of the so-called "summer enrichment program," a 1958 Wisconsin Legislative Council report observed, "this type of program is supported by those who feel the school plant should be used to provide 'extras' to pupils desiring and needing them. It cannot be regarded as a cost-saving device . . . ."; and later, having listed school systems presently operating such programs, the report states they are "not truly all-year schools."[4] On the other hand, the same study found of the four-quarter system that "the main arguments in favor of this plan are that it would help ease the classroom and teacher shortage, and that it would also hold down school costs by obviating the need for new buildings. Current interest has centered on this true all-year plan; and it is strongly urged by advocates of economy in school plant construction and operation."[5]

The absence of a precise definition may also stem from the fact that many so-called all-year school proposals do not entail the year-round attendance of each student. As will be seen from our description of the principal programs, planners of the all-year school primarily address themselves to a "more effective utilization of school facilities." The single unifying characteristic of these proposals, in fact, is the year-round operation of the school plant. In many instances, the student's present nine-month schedule is not essentially disturbed. It can be adjusted and manipulated, but the number of school days for the individual pupil is not necessarily increased.

In essence, then, we use the term "all-year school" here to refer to all those programs which aim at a year-round operation of the school plant and which retain at least some faculty on a twelve-month basis. Within this common aspect there are manifold distinctions, particularly with respect to student schedules.

TYPES OF YEAR-ROUND SCHOOL

As we have concluded, all all-year school patterns imply 12-month operation of the school plant and 12-month employment for at least the majority of the faculty. It is from the perspective of the student schedule, then, that differences emerge. There may be said to be three such principal patterns, each with its variations: the quarter system, the extended semester, and the extended summer session.

The Quarter System

Perhaps the "purest" type of all-year school is the quarter system. As its name implies, it breaks the calendar into four equal increments. There are two separate plans under the quarter system; one a "48-week, four quarter, staggered-vacation school year which allows students to attend three of the four quarters,"[6] and the other "a full 48-week school year in which students attend four quarters of approximately 12 weeks each."[7] Both plans eliminate the conventional summer-vacation pattern and utilize the school facility on a 12-month basis.

The Staggered Quarter. Unlike a compulsory full 48-week school year, the staggered quarter system is a less drastic wrench of traditional school attendance patterns. Under this plan students are divided into four groups, each group attending school three three-month periods with one group absent on vacation each quarter. Teachers have the option of employment for either three or all four quarters, and thus, to an extent, can retain their annual three-month leave if they wish.

Exponents of this system estimate that such a pattern "would achieve a 33.3 per cent economy in school housing. Since three classrooms would do the work of four, each room could accomodate one-third more students—thus lessening the need for, and the financial burden of, new classroom construction."[8] Using the same figures, proponents of the program argue a reduction in the total number of teachers needed. "If only three-fourths of the students were in school at any one time, then only three-fourths as many teachers would be needed as under the nine-month school year system."[9] There is also claimed a corresponding decrease in the number of textbooks required, and for the student an alleviation of crowded conditions.

These statements are not necessarily true, opponents argue. Many factors enter the picture: size of school, preparation of teachers, special service personnel, and so on, they say. Where the staggered quarter has been tried, a 25% decrease in costs has not been documented.

Hence the staggered quarter plan is chiefly debated as an economy measure. In communities where it has been operated, notably in Aliquippa and Ambridge, Pennsylvania, the plan was implemented to answer emergency needs—an immediate shortage of school space and increasing enrollments. Ambridge used the plan to handle its large student body while additional buildings were being constructed. Aliquippa operated the staggered quarter program to avoid investment in new buildings. In each instance, as will be seen later, the need to dictate four equivalent pupil enrollments, with all the attendant administrative complexity, proved formidable. Some school systems investigating the staggered quarter plan discovered that their particular locations rendered the plan infeasible. A committee in Georgia, realizing a considerable investment would have to be made in air-conditioning, stated "the four quarter plan of school operation would cost more than the nine-month/new-plant plan of operation."[10]

Relative to the staggered quarter plan, Donald McCarty has observed, "the assignment of pupils into uniformly equal divisions during the school year, including the assignment of vacation periods, would require arbitrary action on the part of the school authorities."[11] Such a step, of course, involves the administrator in the perilous cross-currents of public opinion. The complication of traditional community life would be significant. Recreational programs, now designed and funded for the summer months, would need adjustment. An arduous reorientation of family patterns could be required. Conceivably parents with large families could have children enrolled in several quarters. In such a case, the family would need to stagger its vacation schedule, and in many instances the situation would be made impossible. In 1952 a National Education Association survey showed that "of all cities over 30,000 in population plus some smaller systems . . . . no city-wide four-quarter plan programs (were) then operating."[12]

The Consecutive Quarter. The full 48-week school year also involves the four quarter system, but there is no involuntary division of students into groups. In this program all the students are in continuous attendance the year-round, with one month of summer allowed as vacation; or the fourth quarter, or summer term, can be offered on a voluntary basis with students and teachers strongly encouraged to participate. Teachers are paid additional salaries. Superior pupils have the privilege of acceleration commensurate with their abilities, and therefore may complete their work earlier. Nashville's consecutive quarter plan was "divided into three terms of twelve weeks each . . . . and an extra term of twelve weeks."[13] Nashville school administrators "interpreted this . . . . to mean that the summer is an integral part of the school year."[14] As in Newark, which operated a similar plan, attendance in the summer term was voluntary.

The advantages of this program, economically, are said to compare with those claimed for the staggered quarter. School facilities are used continuously, teachers are utilized on a twelve-month basis, and the demands of burgeoning enrollments are met without increasing building investment. From an educational point of view, the consecutive quarter plan is said to offer desirable acceleration.

The record is by no means resolved on these points. Granted his motives, "educational rather than economic," the Newark superintendent of schools found his all-year school, operated from 1912 to 1931, to be "eminently successful." The program was abandoned at the onset of the Depression as a way of reducing school costs. Newark, however, now runs summer sessions on elementary and secondary levels, so it would seem educators in that city judge all-year schooling educationally sound. Nashville, on the other hand, discontinued the quarter system after a trial run of five years from 1927 to 1932, and generally regarded the plan unfavorably. No form of year-round school has been revived in that city. Unlike Newark, where enrollment in the summer quarter "was reported as high as 75 per cent,"[15] Nashville found its summer quarter enrollment fluctuating around 50 per cent. Perhaps the element of locality is important in determining the appliance of year-round education. In Newark, "the plan was established in areas populated predominantly with foreign born

. . . . in congested and low-income sections of the city where recreational facilities were lacking."[16] This may explain why Nashville's Negro all-year schools showed higher attendance records in the summer term than the white schools.

In summarizing the demise of both experiments, the U.S. Office of Education is succinct: "They found that graduates of the accelerated programs were too young to secure regular jobs [the Depression years] and not mature enough to enter college. Also they failed to find any economy in such a program."[17]

Both of these dictums have since been rethought to a considerable degree.

Extended Summer Session System

The summer programs, like the four-quarter systems, place the school on a year-round basis of operation. Their main objective, however, is not the reduction of costs. On the contrary, in each instance they call for an increased outlay of funds. Rather, the summer programs seem to pursue purely educational goals: the prevention of loss of learning, enrichment, remedial study, and acceleration. The two types are really variations of a central proposal—the expansion of the conventional summer school into a flexible, experimental summer term which students may volunteer to attend.

Voluntary Faculty. Under one pattern, teachers are continued on a conventional nine-month contract and paid extra to teach such courses as enrollments justify. In essence, the regular school program may be replicated in the summer months, as well as diversified to include courses unsuitable for the formal curriculum. Music appreciation, nature study, and certain crafts are some of the subjects frequently added. Because of its adaptability, the program accelerates bright students on the one hand, offering them advanced courses and experimental projects, and on the other, aids retarded students by providing them remedial classes and specialized attention. An American Association of School Administrators study remarks that "more school systems each year seem to be moving in (this) direction."[18]

Twelve-Month Faculty. Under a modified pattern, all teachers are on 12-month contracts designed "to improve the schools by improving the quality and professional standing of the teachers . . . ."[19] Typical systems work on a five year schedule. Three summers of the five, the teacher works on the curriculum and teaches, one summer he studies, working toward a higher degree. The fifth summer is for vacation and travel. Such a program gives the teacher alternately in summer "instructional chores, a chance to enlarge his experiences through travel, to keep up on pertinent developments in the field of education through study, and to do some of the long-range planning for his classes which is just not possible during the regular school year."[20]

The advantages of these extended summer programs seem clear. In the case of the latter plan, the environment of the teacher is enhanced, and a consequent rise in his standards and performance could follow. Under both plans, the student's participation, as well as the teacher's, is determined by his needs and choice. This flexibility is, of course, attractive, and where the program is presently implemented—for example, Glencoe, Ill., Rochester, Minn., and Lexington, Ky.—communities report their satisfaction with it.

The added costs, of course, are concrete. The Superintendent at Rochester "estimated that about four or five per cent of a $3,000,000 annual budget was used for the summer program, and in Lexington the superintendent reported that 17 or 18 per cent of the annual budget is spent on summer operations."[21]

Extended Semester System

Another type of all-year school pattern is the 210-day school year. As its name implies, it extends the conventional school year to about the middle of July. Teachers are employed on a 12-month basis. In 1961 it was strongly advocated by the

State Superintendent of Schools in Wisconsin, and it seems to be gaining in popularity with other administrators. Called the eleven-month school, a variant type schedules terms from mid August to late January and from late January to late June. Eight weeks of vacation are thus allowed.

A more radical proposal, one that has not gained much response, combines the features of the year-round school with the double-session day. Pupils are in school 4 hours a day for 11 months of the year. Under the proposal teachers work eight hours a day for 11 months, the day evenly divided between teaching, administration, and professional improvement. There are, of course, two shifts of pupils, each having its own group of teachers.

Conceivably, other variations on the central theme will arise as the longer school year is tried under varying conditions.

THE ALL-YEAR SCHOOL IN SONG AND STORY

When we trace the history of the all-year school in America, certain broad trends become apparent. The quarter system was given fairly extensive experimentation roughly from the beginning of this century to the middle years of the Depression. In general the prime motive for implementing the pattern was economy, and when, as they did, the programs seemed to be too expensive, they were discontinued. Following the Second World War, the all-year school has largely been realized through the frame of the extended summer system, and the argument for it has concerned itself chiefly with educational objectives. At no time, in the postwar years, has the four-quarter plan seriously revived. Current studies and analyses, cognizant of the ostensible failures in Newark, Nashville, and Pennsylvania, have concluded an economical four-quarter system to be unworkable, and pursued the contemporary attention to the expanded summer program.

Changing Lay Attitudes

In examining the two periods and two types of all-year experimentation, it becomes clear at the outset that public opinion, over the decades, has changed considerably, evolving from vociferous dissent to acquiescence and, in some cases, to enthusiasm. In 1929 when a proposal for the staggered-quarter plan was aired in Milwaukee, for example, it met with strong protest. The plan was seen variously as a menace to organized labor, since the acceleration of students would glut the labor market, as a threat to the teaching profession, because of its debilitating burdens, and clearly as a disruption of community life. "To figure on how much can be saved by using the school plant the whole year instead of letting it lie idle for a summer period is all very well," the *Milwaukee Journal* editorialized in 1929, "but there is more to the thing than that. Beside the major question of what it will do to the pupils is the very important question of the effect on the home."[22] The *Milwaukee Sentinel* stood duty resolutely: "It is hard for the kindly to cope with logic against the child's love of summer."[23]

The adaptation of the summer school, on the other hand, has proved less troublesome some 50 years later. "In Glencoe (one of the school systems operating the twelve-month faculty plan), a program of extended teacher employment and service has been in successful operation since July 1946."[24] A member of the Lexington Board of Education, summing up public response to their year-round school plan, observed that "in making more of that valuable commodity available to teachers . . . time, the Lexington Board of Education feels that it has made a good investment . . . ."[25] In Milwaukee in 1962, it was the *Journal* and the *Sentinel* who were beating the drums for year-round education, at least at the college and university level. The State Superintendent's call for an extended school year of 210 days received thoughtful consideration both in the press and among interested citizen groups in Wisconsin.

The Quarter Plan Period

Although Bluffton, Indiana, became in 1904 the first public school system to use the quarter plan, the all-year school operated in Newark from 1912 to 1931 has received the most study and seems to have had the greatest impact in educational circles. The features and problems of its program have already been summarized, and will be analyzed in a later section. Generally, local reports favored the continuance of the Newark all-year school, but the importance of locality in such a consideration was underscored. The program rendered "great service, particularly to children of foreign parentage and unfavorable home conditions."[26] One study examined the pattern of juvenile delinquency and related that the all-year school was an important influence "which succeeded in keeping a large proportion of children in the all-year section of Newark out of 'mischief' during the summer."[27] As we shall see, Nashville's all-year school fared less successfully in the minds of its administrators. The Nashville quarter system began in 1927 and ended in 1932, during the Depression which also foreclosed the Newark experiment. Another all-year school system, operated in Omaha, received the praise of its principal in 1925. According to J. H. Beveridge, "the school has been operating 48 weeks a year for about 7 years, and it has proved satisfactory."[28] He added that it was "popular with parents, teachers, and business men."[29] It, too, was stifled in the lean years of the thirties.

Aliquippa's four-quarter plan varied in objective from the Nashville and Newark programs. Referring to them, H. R. Vanderslice, the Aliquippa superintendent, stated, "In all these situations the purpose seems never to have been the fuller use of the school plant."[30] Aliquippa, however, had "the major purpose to utilize fully all existing school buildings before constructing new schools."[31] Ambridge, the second Pennsylvania school system to apply a quarter system, shared with Aliquippa the main purpose "to meet overcrowded conditions." In each instance the quarter plans were enforced because of critical needs and given up when the emergency passed. Aliquippa's staggered quarter plan was in operation from 1928 to 1938 until such time as funds were available for the construction of new schools. Ambridge went on the quarter system only for the duration of its building program and then reverted to the conventional nine-month pattern. Both communities, as will be shown later, found the public hostile to year-round operation. However, Vanderslice noted of the Aliquippa experiment that "although one objection to the all-year school . . . . is that it causes conflicts with the vacations of the parents, one year's experience has fixed our opinion that a smaller number of people go away for extended vacations than is commonly supposed."[32]*

The distinction, then, within the quarter plan period is that the consecutive-quarter programs operated in Newark, Nashville, and Omaha, while seeking the economies of year-round operation, had also envisaged educational goals. Newark, for example, defended the additional cost by citing the advantages of all-year operation for pupils. In the Pennsylvania schools educational gains were not necessarily instrumental in the acceptance of its staggered-quarter plans. These cities, caught in the bind of inadequate appropriations, increasing enrollments, and insufficient school space, turned to the quarter plans primarily as solutions to dire operational problems.

Recent Trends

In the postwar years, as we have already noted, several communities went into year-round operation through the use of the twelve-month faculty plan. In Lexington it seemed strange in 1952 "to think there was a time (and such a long time) when everybody took it for granted children went to school nine months out of twelve and teachers were given nine months' work for nine months' pay."[33]

---

* A statement open to question in reference to the present era.

Still the twelve-month faculty plan, because of its costs, seems not to be swelling into any national tide. Certainly the general attitude has changed, but any broad move toward all-year operation remains in a period of study and calculation.

THE CONTINUING DEBATE

The debate over year-round education at elementary and secondary levels has been really a continuing review and interpretation of its past. Since the War few have been the articles studying all-year operation that did not, in a large part, argue the case from what had happened in Newark or in Aliquippa.

Of Huck Finn and Mr. Chips

What then have been the effects of the all-year school? Certainly the most crucial and unpredictable factor is the student. What has been the effect of continuous attendance on his physical and intellectual stamina? How important is the conventional summer vacation to the pupil? Have the warm summer months actually proved an impediment to class performance? Has he matured sufficiently in his social and emotional development to undertake the responsibilities of adulthood a year earlier than normal matriculation? Do the formulae of year-round operation represent a heavy imposition on the animal vitalities of youth, on his feckless leisure for dreams and self-styled adventure? In the twenties newspapers opposing all-year plans were fond of quoting Whittier and throwing up homely Penrods as barefoot boys bedeviled by frockcoated supercilious adults. Assuredly it takes no effort to imagine Huck Finn's response to the summer term. Unlike his college component who can transfer if he doesn't find the year-round schedule appealing, the eighth grader or the high school sophomore is inexorably bound to whatever system is placed into operation at his school.

To a lesser and yet significant degree this involuntary aspect relates to the elementary and secondary teacher. Many of the questions in year-round education pertinent to school children—the stress of continuous attendance, the effect of the summer months on performance—apply also to him. And yet, though his stake in such programs is high, like the pupil his voice has been negligible in the determination of his fate. In Nashville "with the inauguration of the all-year school, the regular year was reduced to nine months and for the work of the regular year teachers received nine months' salary instead of ten months as heretofore . . . . The effect of this reduction . . . . has been that almost all Nashville teachers . . . . taught each year at least one month in the summer quarter . . . . and that approximately 90 per cent have taught continuously twelve months per year."[34]

Although in recent years the broad situation may have changed, coming as in the case of the twelve-month faculty plan to focus on improved conditions for the teacher, still, in the extensive studies of all-year operation available, there is to be found relatively little mention of the teachers' role. Commentary has almost exclusively derived from the administrative standpoint, dealing primarily with the related student problems: attendance, achievement, and advancement.

Since, then, current studies of year-round operation take as their scripture the results of past experiments, a review of those evaluations is in order. The most impressive documentation exists for the consecutive four-quarter plans operated in Newark and Nashville, and curiously, these analyses generally run counter in their findings.

Newark vs. Nashville

The attitude of one Newark administrator in evaluating the long (1912–1931) Newark experiment with year-round education is commendably practical. "Unless it can be shown indisputably that pupils gain something by attending all-year schools," George Brinkerhoff declared in his 1930 review, "we cannot be certain of the wisdom of operating schools on an all-year basis; and the gains must be sufficient to warrant the expenditure of money necessary for keeping the schools open two extra months each year."[35]

In this regard, how successful was the all-year program? In Newark, as we shall see, the conclusions are glowingly positive, whereas in Nashville the findings are somewhat negative.

Student Health, Physical and Mental? In Newark, it was soundly established that "the fact is . . . . after 18 years of careful observation by teachers and by the medical department in Newark, nothing has been found which would lead anybody to suspect that childrens' health is adversely affected by attending school 12 months a year."[36] Nashville's six-year study of its all-year program concluded similarly, that "there is not the slightest evidence that any child's health has been impaired by attending school during July and August."[37] Generally the Newark studies pair favorably with those done on atypical accelerated elementary and secondary students. Research has shown that superior students at primary levels "showed no significant difference in physical development when compared with the average child. In academic work, they equalled or surpassed their older classmates."[38] Surveying the broad range of studies of acceleration, it was noted that "the research evidence indicated in all the . . . . studies there are no adverse effects from acceleration . . . . The overwhelming evidence still remains in favor of acceleration with positive effects."[39] In Newark, where the poor, average, and bright pupils undertook year-round education together, mutually enduring the presumed 'stress' of summer attendance, the findings have been equally optimistic. They point, moreover, most strongly to the summer term as not only an adequate period for study, but as an excellent and necessary time. "Nor is there any evidence of loss in mental health," the Newark analysis continues. "At the end of summer, after children have been in school 12 months, there are no signs of brain fatigue; and achievement tests given at that time yielded as high ratings as are obtained at any other time of the year."[40] So beneficial did the summer term prove that Newark teachers found their attitudes reversing. "Some teachers had feared that summer schooling would dull pupils' interest in learning, but such did not turn out to be the case. Now many teachers believe that summer study prevents interest from waning."[41]

The Nashville study ambivalently quotes H. C. Weber, a Nashville superintendent, as saying, "students in the summer session, being very earnest and eager to learn, create a wholesome atmosphere for study—discipline is at the zero point,"[42] and then weaves in the theme that "weather conditions at times, it must be confessed, make serious work of any kind next to impossible; neither pupils nor teachers seem to take summer work as seriously as the work of the regular term."[43] (As we shall see, based on the Nashville study's evaluation of summer achievement, it would appear the latter observation is the more verified.)

Student Attendance? In Newark attendance in the summer term was high. "The fact that 75 per cent of the all-year school pupils of Newark return for the summer term, while only 30 per cent of the ten-month pupils . . . . attend summer school, seems to indicate that the children themselves sense the difference in educational values."[44] In Nashville, on the other hand, it was found that "the schools for Negro children have never had in the summer quarter an average daily attendance of less than 59% of the average daily attendance for the three regular quarters and that it has been as high as 69%. In contrast, the average daily attendance in the summer quarter for white children has fallen as low as 41% of the average daily attendance of the regular three quarters, and it has never been above 52%."[45] It is a likely observation that perhaps Nashville's Negro student population more closely resembled in socio-economic status Newark's predominantly immigrant enrollment. Schools which operated on the staggered-quarter basis, Aliquippa and Ambridge, reported favorably on summer attendance. Aliquippa's first quarter (July 15 to October 10) "ranks first in attendance for the five year period."[46] Most significantly, the Aliquippa study found that the quarter which developed the most failures and near-failures and the lowest attendance average was the second quarter (October 10 to January 15), which was "apparently the most unsuitable period of the year for school work, although it is a period of the year . . . . almost universally accepted as school time."[47] H. S. Irons, the Ambridge principal, came to similar conclusions. "The per cent of failures computed on all subject-enrollments during the summer quarter was three and six-tenths. This was lower than any other quarter or semester of the two years."[48] Likewise reflecting the Aliquippa report was the Ambridge findings that its attendance record rose in the summer. Importantly, academic performance was high in their summer quarter.

Student Performance? Newark's eight year analysis showed that the all-year schools graduated 22% more than its ten-month counterparts. "From this one might infer that the holding power of the all-year school is greater and, conversely, that a larger proportion of the pupils of ten-month schools leave school before graduating."[49] Moreover, the average all-year graduate finished his work a half year before the ten-month pupil, and "this shows . . . . a saving of time for all-year pupils."[50] Consequently, "the all-year schools graduate a higher percentage of their pupils; they show a lower grade age; they have less retardation; they lose fewer pupils before graduating."[51] Comparing the all-year pupil with his ten-month counterpart scholastically was a more difficult task. Nevertheless, careful evaluation showed that "the pupils in the all-year schools are further advanced educationally than they would be if they had attended a traditional school instead. Furthermore, the more pupils in the all-year schools have taken advantage of the opportunities offered by the all-year schools, the greater their superiority over comparable traditional pupils."[52]

Conversely the Nashville study showed "the proportion of withdrawals in the summer quarter is practically twice as great as in the fall quarter".[53] Moreover, "a study of the attendance records of 8,957 Nashville pupils in grades 3–8 inclusive for the school year 1928–29, shows that only three pupils out of each hundred attending the summer quarter took vacations during the fall, winter or spring. With these few exceptions, pupils who attend the summer term attend the full year."[54] This means, of course, that the Nashville all-year schools were not necessarily reducing the load on the teacher by spaced enrollments. The study indicated that children who attended the summer quarter and then enrolled for all remaining quarters did so primarily to stay with friends and maintain the traditional pattern of school activity, concluding that their continuous attendance did not for the most part result in grade achievement or speedier matriculation. Two discouraging factors are involved in that estimate. One, "the average per cent of failures for the fourth, fifth and sixth grades for the spring term was 9.4 per cent and for the fall term, 7.8 per cent, whereas for the summer the average per cent of failure was 11.2 per cent,"[55] and two, "in general, approximately three times as many pupils in proportion to the total enrollment drop out before the end of the summer term as drop out during the fall term."[56] Additionally the Nashville researchers discovered in evaluating four comparable groups of Grade 4A pupils that pupils attending "no summer quarters have an average educational age of 129 months, those attending one summer quarter, of 127.6 months, those attending two summer quarters, of 124.9 months, and those attending three summer quarters, 125 months."[57] They concluded "summer conditions in Nashville are probably such . . . . as to make impossible work of as high quality in the summer quarter as in regular quarters."[58]

How alone does Nashville stand in its findings of summer class performance? Although there is no large body of data on the negative effects of summer study, some documentation exists. Ellsworth Huntingdon, the famed climatologist, mentions that "a connection between weather and mental activity appears also when one season is compared with another. A study of Danish schoolchildren long ago led Lehman and Pederson to the hypothesis that there is a mental optimum of temperature considerably lower than the physical optimum . . . . Townsend Lodge, for example, has found that intelligence tests of the same person vary according to season.

When four groups of children from superior social and economic backgrounds . . . . were given four successive tests at six month intervals, the average group ratings between November and April "were invariably higher than when the same children were tested between May and October."[59] Another investigation of the relationship between barometric pressure and relative humidity and the categories of classroom behavior revealed that "restless, 'squirmy' behavior may be related to a combination of high relative humidity and low barometric pressure,"[60] and suggested climatic variables be considered in behavioral analysis. An earlier evaluation of weather effects which marked behavioral patterns against daily weather readings in a group of New York City public schools noted that "it will be seen that cold, calm and clear days are those on which deportment and work are generally considered to be at their best . . . . for 'Worst' condition, muggy days take the lead . . . ."[61] Moreover, class work followed the graph bar of behavior closely, falling in hot weather, rising in cold weather. Studying school attendance charts culled from school systems both in New York and Denver, the analysis asserted "the de-energizing effects of the high humidities accompanied by high temperatures are recognized."[62]

These citations would seem to support the Nashville report, and yet the favorable accounts of summer study at Newark and the Pennsylvania schools should not be neglected. There is then no clear-cut reply to the criticism that the warm summer months are toxic to the child's learning. On the other hand, both the Nashville and Newark studies agree that continuous attendance has not resulted in nervous strains or mental fatigue. Physically the summer term seems not to impose stress.

Student Maturity? It is a more arduous problem to assess the maturity of the all-year school graduate in comparison to his traditional-school fellow. The respected Farrand and O'Shea analysis of the Newark all-year school deflated the issue by observing "there is only a negligible difference between the ages of graduation of all-year when compared with traditional school pupils."[63] As it has been shown, the average Newark all-year graduate matriculated a half-year earlier. Certainly acceleration to this degree seems not significant. Even where all-year schools accelerate pupils one to two years earlier, it would be difficult to determine in the mass any charge of immaturity. What, for example, is the deciding criterion, the dividing line between adulthood and adolescence? Critics should be able to spend several decades formulating a standard.

Missing Ingredients? It is also difficult to assess what might be called the "lyrical" qualities of the summer vacation. In Newark and Nashville where only the streets were available for summer experience, undeniably the summer term has particular utility. But in other communities where streams and woods and capacious parks are nearby, the question of summer study involves more than the practical aspects. We spoke briefly of Huck Finn and the leisure for dreams. The junior author of this study remembers warmly the indolence of his summer vacations and the supreme joy of being able to avoid supervision. Perhaps it is or could be important for young boys not to have their recreation flawlessly charted. Regretfully this is a matter hard to document. Possibly children won't miss what they've never had. Certainly the summer enrichment programs or extended summer sessions have proved popular with pupils, but they do not, of course, involve for the most part full academic loads and involuntary participation.

Teacher Morale? There appears to have been no extensive investigation of the teachers' role in all-year operation, and yet many of the objectives stated for it involve the teacher: his better utilization, and the necessity of increasing his salary. Under the quarter plans it is evident that the administrative view prevailed. Regarding the staggered-quarter program, one study optimistically suggested, "if only three fourths of the students were in school at any one time, then only three fourths as many teachers would be needed as under the nine month school system.[64] Another source saw possible relief for the personnel problem through the agency of year-round operation. "With full-time employment for teachers and better annual salaries, the teacher-turnover problem will be less serious."[65] H. S. Irons, Ambridge principal, remarked that "the new plan (the staggered quarter) reduced the number of teachers needed from 69 to a quarterly average of 57."[66]

Undoubtedly the attraction of twelve-month employment with its attendant salary increase is strong for the generally low-salaried teacher. In the post-war years, however, the idea of improving the cost and use of the teacher has changed somewhat, through the twelve-month faculty plan, to focus as well on his development. P. J. Misner, Glencoe principal, has noted the additional benefit of in-service training available within the plan. The flexible summer session can be used for the introduction of new teachers to a new school system. The concept of the 30% pay raise for year-round teaching prevalent under the quarter systems as inducement enough seems to have favorably broadened its impact.

Quality of Instruction? What, however, were the effects of teaching year-round under the quarter plans? Only brief mention is made in the appropriate studies. Under the consecutive-quarter plan, the Nashville report makes no mention of mental or psychological exhaustion on the part of its teachers. Brinkerhoff's thorough analysis of the Newark all-year school parenthetically adds that in relation to the teacher "there is no evidence to prove that summer work, or that twelve months' work a year, has been harmful."[67] H. R. Vanderslice, principal of Aliquippa's staggered quarter plan, observed that "no protest against the plan has been heard. Several teachers in the schools with sessions in nine months have applied for positions in the all-year schools, and more applications from teachers outside the district were received during the past year than ever before."[68] Similarly the Ambridge principal noted of his staggered quarter system that "teachers' health and attendance comparison covering the two years revealed . . . . little or no difference in the per-teacher frequency of personal illness."[69] He added that a large majority of his staff "very frankly stated that they considered the plan a success."[70]

No mention is made, however, pertinent to level of performance. Without accompanying evidence, the Nashville study insinuated that the quality of instruction lagged in the summer term. Whether the inference is drawn from the relatively inferior academic achievement of Nashville's summer quarter student or is based on direct observation is not made clear. It should also be pointed out that the apparent success of the twelve-month faculty plan has been scored in school systems where the socio-economic background of the pupils is perhaps higher than the national average. An elementary and secondary teacher practicing his art in a depressed area, stymied by negative sociological pressures and harrassed by disciplinary problems, might logically demand his three-month leave, and both deserve and require it. Significantly a 1959 New York State Teachers Association resolution frowned severely on any loss of the conventional three-month summer absence through arbitrary measures.

Nevertheless, schools which operated quarter plans and employed their teachers year-round did not report serious difficulties. To the contrary, based on the slim evidence available, it appears teachers have functioned as well year-round as in nine months, and in some cases, as in Newark, were reportedly stimulated by the program. Nashville is again the notable exception.

Administrative Headaches? It is not, at any rate, the presence of teacher stress and the seasonal fluctuation of his performance that have preoccupied recent studies of year-round operation. Foremost of the objections to the quarter plans, particularly the staggered quarter, has been the requirement for delicate and complicated administration.

In 1951 *The Nation's Schools* ran a survey of school administrators on the topic of the all-year school. Earlier that year an Illinois Taxpayers' Federation had proposed editorially in the Chicago *Daily News* that the staggered quarter plan be revived. The survey found that "less than 10%"[71] of the administrators thought such a program advisable. The reasons of the dissident majority were broad. Primarily they were apprehensive of the administrative implications, rightly fearing the difficulty of controlling enrollments. On the other hand, the survey revealed that a great number still clung to the antique disadvantages. "Summer, first of all, is not conducive to study."[72] Additionally "teachers need the time to rest from the mental and emotional strain."[73] Supplementary problems were discovered. A Colorado superintendent questioned the effect on the tourist business "if one-fourth of the families couldn't travel."[74] In fact, surprising special interests considered themselves involved. *The Journal of Health, Physical Education, Recreation* in a January, 1961 symposium, "Should the School Year Be Lengthened?" cautiously wondered if recreational programs now funded directly by the municipality might be subsumed, and perhaps shabbily treated, by the general school budget.

In 1955 *The Nation's Schools* repeated the poll and found the position of the superintendents on the staggered quarter relatively unchanged. Seventy-two per cent replied unfavorably. Administration was still regarded as a central problem, and reasons of increased maintenance costs were also offered. The superintendents pointed out that, contrary to current thought on the elementary and secondary calendar, there remained a substantial number of areas in the U. S. where pupils were still needed in the harvest fields in summer. They indicated, too, that many school districts simply could not afford the salary increases and increased costs of operating their schools year-round. The survey concluded by arguing for "at least some middle ground between the two extreme positions of complete rejection or complete acceptance."[75]

Economy? What has been the record of economy for the quarter plans, and does it justify the administrative complexity? The respected Farrand and O'Shea analysis of Newark's all-year school found "that the added schooling given by the all-year schools . . . . costs the city of Newark less than one sixtieth of the total school budget, which seems to be but a small item and should not weigh heavily in determining whether the all-year school should be continued."[76] Nashville, however, disclosed "an increase of instructional cost of $105,-164.28 or twenty-one per cent"[77] in its first year of year-round operation. As for the summer term, "it cost $6.48 or 64 per cent more for instruction per pupil in average daily attendance for the summer quarter than for the regular quarters."[78] A Newark study concluded that "it cost Newark in the period, 1913 to 1923, $561.89 for the all-year school to graduate one student and $800.00 for the ten-month school."[79] Under the staggered quarter system, Lyle Wilson, superintendent of the Aliquippa school, is quoted as saying, "We saved about $40,000 a year over the seven years covered by this study."[80]

The staggered-quarter plan, since it readily answers teacher and school facility shortages, has received some serious consideration. In Aliquippa it did result in a more efficient use of existing physical plant and eased the burden of increasing enrollments. Bearing this in mind, a 1953 article in the journal, *School Executive*, suggested the staggered quarter as a stopgap measure, concluding nonetheless that "as an ultimate pattern it would probably be unsound. However, we are faced with an immediate problem."[81] The article took note of supplementary problems. "The quarter plan would make athletic eligibility a headache for coaches and administrators, and to some extent create a problem for those music teachers who engage in competitive interscholastic activities."[82] Certainly, "the maintenance and repair of school buildings would present a problem since most major repairs and redecoration takes place during the summer vacation period."[83] Another critic of the staggered-quarter plan noted "a new group of students every three months would mean a multiple class situation for each teacher and thus impair the instruction program."[84] Reviewing past experiments with the staggered quarter, the American Association of School Administrators at its 1958 regional conventions concluded that "forty or more numerous and formidable administrative problems inherent in the plan, plus the fact that the actual number of school days for each pupil would be slightly reduced below the customary 175–180 days, make the adoption of the four-quarter plan impractical and unwise."[85] Still, it is observed that "the nine month school year . . . . hardly seems to fill the bill now."[86]

Public and Professional Acceptance? What should so strongly stamp this unfavorable impression of the quarter plans? It has been seen that generally these programs accomplished their goals and resulted in neither drastic misfortune for the pupil nor bad conditions for the teacher. Considerable economies were reported.

Robert Crawford noted of the Aliquippa all-year school that "the outstanding disadvantage of the all-year school was the refusal of the public to accept the plan. Many families claimed that their vacation plans were ruined . . . . At one time a few employees of the Jones & Laughlin Steel Company were told to send their children to school when scheduled or to find another job."[87] H. C. Hartsell quotes an Ambridge administrator as saying "the plan was extremely difficult to administer, unpopular with the parents, and discontinued as soon as new buildings were completed."[88]

The administrative implications of the operational dicta established by the Research Division of the National Education Association should be recalled. "In order to have reasonable efficiency," the study states, "the pupil enrollment would have to be divided into four equal groups. Not only should the total enrollment of pupils be the same for each quarter, but the number enrolled in each grade in the elementary school and in each subject in the high school should be approximately the same during each quarter."[89] It adds that "unless the enrollment is sufficiently large enough to permit teacher-pupil ratios as efficient as the ratios maintained in the normal plan of operation, the per-pupil costs tend to go up rather than down. Furthermore, a four quarter distribution likely would result in less efficient bus loads, more months of employment for transportation personnel, and a consequently greater salary expenditure."[90] Certainly the arbitrary nature of these requirements appear burdensome to the already stiffly worked elementary and secondary administrator.

The feeling that the conventional nine-month school pattern is now inadequate seems to be growing in the minds of administrators. Models for extended school years, however, have come in no sudden rush, nor have there been proposed suitable variations of the now-historic quarter plans. Although the twelve-month faculty plans have proved successful, the fact that in Lexington "the financing of the plan required a 20% increase in the tax rate"[91] undoubtedly detracts from its allure. "The trend," one source indicated, "is toward a longer school year organized on a single term or two-semester basis and supplemented by more extensive summer programs."[92] D. O. Clark in the *School Executive* observed in 1958 that "the 12-month program, with four groups of children following four different schedules and with alternating vacations, has been found to bring about more administrative confusion and parental ill will than expected economies."[93] He proposed "the 11-month school year would eliminate the added management problems of the four-quarter promotions, staggered programming, record-keeping by quarters."[94] In a sense, then, the 210-day school is a year-round operating alternative.

HIGHLIGHTS AND SIDELIGHTS

From this brief look at elementary and secondary all-year school patterns, what can we say are the cardinal problems and prospects, as revealed by reasoning and research?

At the outset, it seems clear it is extremely hazardous to generalize about the all-year school. Each type, even each sub-type, has its peculiar advantages and disadvantages, particularly in terms of geographic setting and milieu.

Let us consider first the matter of economy. There is little question that the extended summer session and extended semester versions will add to a school's operating budget without any accompanying saving in capital investment. The quarter systems, on the other hand, have the inherent capability to produce economies, but only in the presence of enrollment controls that border on police action. Both patterns achieve increased utilization of school facilities, of course.

In terms of educational goals, the quarter systems and the extended semester emphasize acceleration, for better or worse. The extended summer session offers specialized enrichment and review, in addition to acceleration. Again for better or worse, both patterns tend to place faculty on a 12-month basis.

The consecutive quarter system, the Newark experience suggests, has a hidden ability to combat juvenile delinquency. On the other hand, the Nashville trial suggests this pattern may have serious drawbacks in the South in the absence of air-conditioned classrooms. The quarter systems may be better adapted to urban areas, the flexible summer session to rural regions. Certainly the latter pattern is less disruptive of family and community living.

The observation of Newark's Brinkerhoff that "the holding power of the all-year school is greater" may have relevance to the current alarming national incidence of high school dropouts. The connection may be statistically tenuous, but the all-year school could be a remedy. In Newark, a modern industrial city, all-year schools, drawing from the low-income groups, comparatively held and graduated more pupils than their 10-month counterparts. The problem, of course, is that Newark's all-year school was pre-war, and social vagaries being what they are, the relevance may not still exist. Still, the facts are to be pondered. The New Yorks and Chicagos, with their crowded employment offices, might take a second look at the admirable attendance records of Newark and Aliquippa, and envy Newark's retention and graduation of all-year pupils.

On one aspect of the all-year school it seems safe to generalize; namely, with respect to student and faculty performance in summer. Most of the available evidence suggests that summer study and teaching are not necessarily debilitating; indeed, the opposite can be true. Yet it is equally sure the emotional opposition to summer work has scarcely abated.

What emerges from our reconnaissance is simply this: that, given an over-riding objective, an American community can find a school pattern that will meet its needs, but no one pattern will solve all problems. If a community places top priority on economical physical plant utilization, for example, a quarter system can attain it, but only at the expense of major changes in conventional school and family living patterns. If, on the other hand, a community wants educational offerings of top quality and quantity, the extended summer session offers a flexible framework that does not necessarily disrupt going school and community practices, but the added cost will be measurable. Hence it will be unlikely that we will see emerge a standard all-year school pattern, and the resulting lack of integration with sister institutions may in itself create new problems.

Suffice it to say that as American citizens debate the pros and cons of the all-year school in the years ahead, the resulting dialogue between professionals and public can enhance our whole educational system, provided we deal with philosophies rather than with prejudices, and with fact rather than fancy.

THE SITUATION TODAY

Depending on how you define the term "year-round school," American elementary and secondary education is either moving away from, or toward, an extended calendar. Early in American history, an 1841 government study suggests, 11-month calendars could be found in use in such city schools as Baltimore, Buffalo, Cincinnati, Detroit, New York, Philadelphia, and Washington. By 1900 the 180-day year had become fairly standard, but all-year calendars cropped up again in the '20s, in such cities as Ardmore and Tulsa, Oklahoma; Chattanooga and Nashville, Tennessee; Newark, New Jersey; El

Paso, Texas; Elveleth, Minnesota; Gary, Indiana; Ma
Iowa; Minot, North Dakota; and Omaha, Nebraska.
War II sparked considerable discussion about continuo
endars; Lexington, Kentucky, however, was one of the few cities actually to adopt the pattern, and that city closed its year-round schedule four years ago. Today only one public school is known to be following a four-quarter schedule—the Florida State University Laboratory School.

Thus, despite the emergence of a National School Calendar Study Committee and its propaganda about idle plants, loss of teacher services, and taxpayer revolts against rising expenditures for public education, full year-round operation at the elementary and secondary level is not catching on. The reason why is probably because families accustomed to having their children out of school during the summer do not look favorably on year-round attendance. Editorial Research Reports states the situation succinctly:

"Many parents feel that other summer activities—camp or family vacations—provide experiences as necessary to child growth as formal education. The suggestion that children might continue to attend school for the usual nine months but take vacations on a staggered schedule likewise meets with disfavor. Parents with more than one child would find it impossible to take family vacations unless their children were all free at the same time. Even if there were no question of going away from home, they wonder what they would do with children on vacation during a season when weather frequently forbids outdoor play and sports."[95]

If the quarter system appears dead at the moment, the summer session system is quite another matter. The American Association of School Administrators reported in 1960 that "more school systems each year seem to be moving in the direction of extending the school program into the summer months."[96] A concurrent survey by the National Education Association reported that 92 per cent of cities with populations of more than 500,000, and four-fifths of cities with more than 30,000 population had summer schools with sessions of from four to 10 weeks. Editorial Research Reports said in 1963 that summer attendance is growing faster than total school enrollment.[97] A Virginia educator concludes that "as the world's knowledge increases and it becomes more and more imperative that we utilize to the fullest possible extent the time and talents of both children and teachers, not to mention making the fullest possible use of an enormously expensive educational plant, we will move toward a longer school year."[98]

But perhaps it is left to another Virginia educator, Thomas Jefferson, to summarize the situation. We cannot always do what we might want to do, he told the embryo University of Virginia. Those for whom we act have their own rights and powers. To do to our fellow men the most good in our power, we must lead where we can, follow where we cannot, "and still go with them."

III

The Year-Round College and University

LIKE THE elementary and secondary school, the American college began life as a creature of the agricultural calendar—only in reverse. Harvard during its first 100 years operated on a four-term calendar which began in mid-August and ended with graduation in mid-July. A long winter vacation allowed college students to teach in the lower schools. This general pattern persisted across the country until well past the Civil War. With the democratization of higher education and the rise of graduate study and research, the fall-spring semester calendar became dominant at the turn of the century, and the summer was limited increasingly to specialized programs of teaching and investigation.

In the present day, it is not unusual for a university to play host in summer to more individuals than it does in winter. Nor is it unusual for as many research projects to be brought to fruition in July as in January. In this sense, then, the typical American university can be said to be operating now on a year-round basis. But it is equally true that such summer instructional programs generally will be of comparatively short duration, from two days to 10 weeks, so that in terms of fall and winter occupancy, campus facilities are seldom occupied to their maximum in summer. Dr. John Dale Russell, a specialist in space utilization studies, told the Committee on Higher Education in New York State in 1960 that if classrooms were used to the greatest extent possible during the day and evening and all through the year, present classrooms could handle four times the present number of students. (There are numerous and formidable obstacles in the way of theoretically perfect utilization of space, of course, some of which are deeply embedded in academic tradition.)

Meanwhile higher education was being deluged. The United States Office of Education has reported that the degree-credit enrollments during the academic year 1961–62 amounted to 3,891,000 students, an increase of 32 per cent above the figures reported in 1956. Forecasts of future enrollments vary somewhat, but few informed persons doubt that by 1970 at least seven million young people in this country will be seeking some type of higher education. These sharply rising enrollments will place unprecedented burdens on the faculties and facilities of colleges and universities.

This Associated Press dispatch (in mid-November of 1962) tells the story in dramatic fashion:

> Higher education is bursting at the seams all over the country.
>
> From the smallest private colleges to the great, sprawling state universities, the current academic year is marked by change and innovation.
>
> The tide of change and innovation is running strong, and every college in the land has been caught up in the current.
>
> The one, main, over-riding reason is the force of numbers.
>
> According to a *New York Times* survey, 58.6 per cent of all the 1962 high school graduates had planned to enter college this fall, including a fantastic 70.7 per cent of the young men and 47.4 per cent of the young women.
>
> When all the figures are in, total college enrollment for 1962–63 is expected to reach 4,729,000. This includes 450,000 in two-year junior colleges and 790,000 taking college courses without credit toward a degree.
>
> This is another in a long string of record enrollments but, a entertainer Al Jolson used to say, "Folks, you ain't seen nothin' yet!"
>
> The first crop from the post-war baby boom won't start pounding on college doors until 1964. And by that time, as many as 70 per cent of all high school graduates may well be demanding a higher education.
>
> In the face of such pressure no college, public or private, can remain static; all will have to change to meet the changing times.

Seeing idle halls with one eye and mushrooming educational needs with the other, some educational planners, both professional and lay, have shown increased interest in recent years in a year-round university operation that would increase campus and faculty utilization in summer. For some, the primary objective has been economy; for others, enriched educational offerings and accelerations. All concerned have pointed with "it can be done" fingers to the widespread experimentation with year-round education practiced by colleges and universities during World War II.

The following recent *Chicago Tribune* story is typical of the calendar ferment on today's college campus:

> Springfield, Ill., Jan. 23 (1963)—A trimester (three term) plan, which possibly would go into effect in 1965, has been recommended by a University of Illinois study subcommittee, it was learned today.
>
> The report was submitted by a group headed by John Cribbett, professor of law, and it will go before faculty and university staff committees for further study.
>
> Under the proposed plan, a full summer term will be added to the two semesters presently offered.
>
> Several advantages to a trimester plan were cited by the subcommittee. The state would be able to use its costly buildings and physical plant on a year-around basis. Students who could not enter in September would be able to start in January. Some also would decide to wait and start in the summer.
>
> University officials expect a tremendous load of new students by 1965, when youngsters born in the post-war "baby-boom" year of 1947 will be entering college. A trimester plan would make it possible for the university to handle more students.
>
> Additional faculty members and faculty officers would have to be added to handle the increased load under the trimester plan, said Lyle Lanier, provost, Lanier said university officials would not expect faculty members to assume a heavier load to implement the plan.
>
> Costs of the plan were not mentioned in the report by the subcommittee.
>
> "We do not have any money for this in our budget request for 1963–65," Lanier said, "However, we did plan for a projected increase in enrollment in this period."
>
> The proposal recommended by the Cribbett subcommittee is patterned after a plan prepared to go into effect at the University of Michigan, Lanier said.

Under this plan there would be a split third term in which a student could choose to go either the full 15 weeks or take a condensed course in 7½ weeks. The same amount of classwork would be involved in both systems.

All told, some 40 institutions, as of January 1963, had established formal calendars for operating their campuses on a year-round basis. All permit the student who desires to do so to earn his B.A. degree in three rather than the usual four calendar years (or to earn a B.A. in a work-study program, or a master's degree in a shorter period of time than would otherwise be possible) without requiring him to carry more than a "normal" full-time course load. This yardstick sets off the 40 colleges and universities from a much more numerous group of institutions that offer traditional summer sessions. Institutions of all sizes and types are represented. These are the institutions whose administrators see their calendars as a means of encouraging students to attend year-round. In some other institutions, students can work out year-round attendance on their own.[3]

The State Senate of Pennsylvania was so impressed with the year-round plan at Pittsburgh, Penn State, and a Pennsylvania state teachers' college that it passed a resolution commending these institutions "for their forward-looking approach in making their facilities available to a larger number of students by instituting 12-month programs."[4]

Arrayed against the innovators is an impressive jury of educational planners, again both professional and lay, who see in year-round education the introduction of more problems than it allays. They are abetted by the fact that most all-year calendars are in the developmental stage, with many attendant matters yet to be worked out, such as integration of the college calendar with high school graduation dates, the amount of tuition to be charged, the faculty salary formula, the total teaching load, the range of programs to be offered, how to set up the proper sequence of courses, how to arrange for the needs of school teachers taking abbreviated summer programs, and how to integrate ROTC summer camp activities. Moreover, a comprehensive evaluation of faculty and student attitudes is still to be made at most institutions.[5]

Hence, as in the case of the all-year school debate at the elementary and secondary level, any current discussion of the year-round university is apt to generate as much heat as light. Both sides tend to be cavalier in their use of terms and statistics. In this chapter we attempt a dispassionate description of the situation.

THE STARTING POINT

By Way of Definition

While those institutions offering truncated summer terms may say they are operating on a year-round basis, more precisely the term *year-round education* has come to signify an academic calendar approaching "either three semesters per year or four quarters per year."[6] Under such a system, the university operates comprehensively on a year-round schedule, utilizing its physical plant, administration, and faculty fully or nearly so, in each of the terms. Unlike the conventional summer session, which "evolved"[7] from teacher institutes into the complex multifaceted programs of today, the additional third semester or fourth quarter running through the summer months is completely integrated into the regular academic pattern. Presumably *it is* a regular term, and in context and clientele does not differ markedly from the traditional winter and spring terms.

Popularly the pattern is understood as a means of student acceleration and better use of facilities. Students graduate in three rather than four years, and cherished funds are not dissipated in the empty air of idle classrooms, proponents point out. To legislators, whose responsibilities include their extensive state systems of higher education, with anticipated increases in student registrations (for example, by 1971 the state of Wisconsin expects to double its present enrollment, from 73,117 to 132,290)[8] and their necessary consequence of increased costs, the ready and available solution often appears to be some form of year-round education. Recently a year-round educational program was arbitrarily legislated in Florida, and governors elsewhere have taken to calling for year-round calendars.

On the other hand, university administrators and faculties, mindful of various pressures, regard year-round education from a number of viewpoints. Accordingly, academic opinion is diversified. "The administrator has been the prime mover in making decisions for year-round operation. While the faculty is included at some point in the planning, their lack of perspective on the total situation, their limited concern for special disciplines, and their emotional involvement usually mean that the impetus for radical calendar change is given by executive decision."[9] Hence year-round education, varied mechanically in itself, is as much a target as a topic. Moreover, as David McKenna has amply suggested, while year-round education may be "an inevitable part of the future for most colleges and universities,"[10] the present period is one of transition and experimentation.

By Way of Background

All such transitions start from two conventional calendars, the semester and the quarter.

The Semester Calendar. The most broadly used system at present, the semester pattern, is "generally composed of two regular terms of about 16 weeks of classes each, running from late September to early June, plus a summer session which is outside the regular academic pattern."[11] In its complicated arrangement of intra-term breaks and holidays, the semester system involves a "lame-duck" session, a brief period of classes usually from one to two weeks left in the first term which protrudes, past the Christmas recess, into the new year.

Advocates of the semester calendar, vexed with the inconvenience of this feature, have proposed a number of revisions with the aim of preserving the basic pattern of the semester. One such plan[12] envisaged a division of six periods of eight weeks each, which, although it tightened considerably the student's schedule and intensified the work load of the faculty, did not represent "at bottom much more than transformation of our two semester plus summer session program."[13] Period I, July–August, is compared with the summer session. Period VI, May–June, is regarded as the most innovative, since it could be skipped by job-hunting students and used primarily for special studies. One indication of this particular study, compiled by faculty members, may be the apparent reluctance of many faculty to dispense with the semester pattern. This particular study emphatically ruled out, at any rate, the three-term and four-quarterly plans, programs most generally associated with year-round education. As the booklet, *The University Calendar,* indicates, by its very extensive operation the semester "can be considered as empirically satisfactory."[14] Whether its utility, confronted with a burgeoning mass of students, will continue to be applicable is the doubted premise of most calendar studies.

The Quarter Calendar. "The quarter system is composed of three regular terms per year with about ten weeks per term in instructional time and a school year of about the same overall length as under a semester system (typically 37 or 38 weeks), running from late September to early June. The fourth quarter is generally a summer session period outside the regular academic program and with a different emphasis."[15] As of January 1, 1960, "14% (of 1,058 regionally accredited colleges and universities) were on the quarter system."[16] Although it solves some of the schedule inequities of the semester system (the lame-duck session, for example), the quarter plan involves administrative complications (it starts and ends terms more frequently); and there is doubt among many educators of the merit of its short spans of course learning.

All year-round education plans are basically extensions of these two college calendar patterns.

FORMS OF YEAR-ROUND EDUCATION

Four-Quarter System

The universities and colleges which have been operating on a three-quarter-plus-summer-term pattern have practically no transitional problem if they wish to move to a full-scale year-round calendar. All they need do is expand their summer term until it approximates in length and offerings those of a winter increment. Some universities, notably Ohio State, have been operating under such a pattern for many years. Indeed, in at least one quarter-system university, Colorado, the summer term enrollment has actually approached that of the fall term.

Semester-Quarter Version

The university or college which starts from the semester pattern and moves to a quarter plan has problems in equating credits, tailoring courses, and adjusting faculty loads. A compromise is the Pennsylvania State semester-quarter pattern. In 1960 Penn State moved from a two-semester calendar to a four-term system, each term consisting of ten weeks. Class periods were increased from 50 to 75 minutes to attain the number of minutes of instruction available under the old 15-week semester schedule. The four terms were made equivalent in curriculum and credit structure, and fees were divided equally. "Any short-term offerings for teachers," it was planned, would be "handled in a concurrent separate summer session."[17] The utility of the summer session, with the meat of its academic program transferred to the regular summer term, becomes, however, questionable. Pittsburgh, in its trimester program, has encountered difficulty in its parallel operation of a summer session and term, and, as we shall see, the Easton analysis of year-round operating schedules urges that for maximum efficiency "summer activities such as conferences, symposia, and short courses"[18] be given up if any savings are to be realized.

Penn State's new academic calendar was caused by three main requirements: the needs of a "more flexible program of studies . . . of the rapidly increasing number of students . . ." and ". . . the year-round utilization of the resources of the University."[19]

These motives, which receive recurrent stress in the literature on year-round education, vary in respective emphasis from school to school, but their repetition nationally makes them the cardinal principles of such calendar changes. At Penn State, the semester-quarter plan is the represented solution to them. Problems, however, remain. There is an enrollment-crippled summer session to maintain. Students find an increased flexibility in the schedule, more frequent re-entry and acceleration, recesses falling between terms, and fewer courses per term period; administrators hopefully reap savings stemming from all-year operation. Yet there are distinctive stresses in faculty adjustment. While "the salary of a faculty member for teaching three terms will be the same as is now paid for two semesters,"[20] the teacher finds himself with unique responsibilities. "Departments," a local memorandum points out, "need to study carefully what to offer during each term so as to permit forward progress of students who are attempting to complete studies in three years as well as the students who would complete in four years."[21] Moreover, the nettlesome task of adjusting teaching time and off-term leave remains to be figured annually on an individual basis. (Shippensburg State College, Pennsylvania, also has inaugurated year-round education on the four-quarter plan, but its schedule differs in that terms are set at 12 weeks. Classes, moreover, run from early morning until the late evening.)

The Trimester

The university traditionally operating on a semester system can also move to year-round education via the so-called trimester pattern. The trimester, actually "three semesters", is composed of three 15-week terms.

The trimester pattern operated at the University of Pittsburgh has received considerable publicity at the national level, and many educators regard it as a pivotal experiment. Acceleration, the increased handling of increasing numbers of students, has been a persistent theme in Pittsburgh's calendar deliberations. "Possibly the greatest single impediment to a liberal and professional education," the Assistant Chancellor at Pittsburgh asserted in reviewing the Pittsburgh trimester, "is the length of time required under the traditional calendar."[22]

The Philosophy. The concept of early matriculation following an uninterrupted academic pace, however, is not a new one. As early as 1900, C. W. Eliot, then president of Harvard, was proposing that the "whole school life should be one unbroken flow. . . ."[23] More recently, in an article in *The Saturday Evening Post,* Grayson Kirk, president of Columbia, crystallized these attitudes. Echoing the Pittsburgh position, Dr. Kirk noted that "the most insistent problem in higher education today is the necessity to reduce the time spent in preparing for careers."[24] Acceleration, he said, is surely needed, and the logical remedy "is the trimester plan."[25] Illustrating his preference, Kirk stated that the trimester plan "promotes better student attitudes toward the serious business of acquiring an education"[26] because the student must "buckle down to three years of hard work" rather than "breezing through in four years."[27] The severity of his words, reflecting the viewpoint that the leisurely pace of four years causes scholastic crimes in the curriculum, 'snap courses' and the like, and creates for the student an unfavorable excess of time in which to idle, can perhaps be related to another philosophy. What Kirk wants basically is a heavy increase in the student's responsibility for his own education. Reflecting this point of view, there has been a growing emphasis in American education on the "shift from teaching to learning."[28] This trend was articulated in the report, "An Educational Program for Dartmouth," prepared by a joint Faculty and Board of Trustees Committee at Dartmouth in 1956.

"Suppose," the report speculated, "the focus is shifted from teaching to learning, and colleges begin to think of their task as one of enabling students to learn without being taught."[29] The consequences in student-teacher relations are regarded as being enormously complicated, and the need to intensify faculty impact correspondingly becomes primary. The Dartmouth proposals began with the adoption of a trimester, and subsequent revisions—independent reading programs, modifications of humanities and science requirements—fanned out beneath it. The emphasis, as Dr. Kirk declared, needs to be turned from the "playpen" atmosphere of the conventional university calendar to the more rigorous and concentrated demands of the trimester plan. The student must commit himself completely to his education. The position, and indeed the problem, of the student will be discussed later. Mention of him at this point is made only to underline the thinking of college administrators when they cite as a prime reason for trimester calendars, "the need for a more flexible program of studies,"[30] and the resolution of the conflict between "generalized education and specialized knowledge."[31] Ostensibly, then, the change to year-round education means a basic change in the attitude of the educator toward the student.

Not all educators, of course, are entranced with the philosophy of increased emphasis on "learning" if it implies decreased emphasis on "teaching." As one such professor has put it, "Students should not be forced to go out in canoes without lifebelts."

The desire to intensify the student's responsibility for his education was central in Pittsburgh's calendar study, and played a significant role in that university's rejection of the quarter system because it "would be much less likely than a trimester arrangement to change students' attitudes toward summer study."[32] The fourth quarter, it was suspected, would lapse into the conventional image of the summer school. Pittsburgh envisaged, on the contrary, a thorough revolution of its academic pattern. The fixed idea of summer as a rest period, in order to make their program successful, needed complete banishment.

The need to quicken the academic pace of the student, to heighten the climate of his education, while simultaneously providing space and time for additional numbers was not the only factor which led Pittsburgh to the trimester. Indeed, the better utilization of plant facilities is omnipresent in considerations of the trimester, and figured significantly in the case of Pittsburgh. As it "estimated that the 12-month calendar will cut the need for facilities by 40%,"[33] the investigating committee kept in mind that "about 35% of the University of Pittsburgh budget is needed whether students are present or not; this part of the budget is made up of debt service, plant, books, administrative staff, service staff, etc., and is required whether students are present 9 or 11 months."[34]

The Mathematics. In 1958, the year Pittsburgh decided on the pattern of its new calendar, a Rutgers College of Engineering statistical analysis of year-round calendars, under the direction of Elmer Easton, was published. It examined a number of operating schedules and determined the trimester to be the optimal program in terms of efficiency and cost. The particular trimester developed by Easton, while mathematically feasible, imposes nevertheless operational restrictions which are nearly impossible to enforce. Basically the system calls for "three 16 week terms per calendar year"[35] with student classes rotating two out of the three terms. The calendar would admit in each term, and approximately four weeks would be set aside for vacations and holidays. Under this plan, Easton envisages universities could "grant 56% more degrees per year, make up to 30% more use of the instructional facility, and increase faculty salaries approximately 30%."[36] But to accomplish this feat, the administration would have "to give up summer activities such as conferences, symposia, and short courses, alter the traditional pattern of starting time and vacation period for students, reduce faculty vacations to four weeks, and enforce uniform distribution among several entering classes per year."[37] The chief difficulty, other than the disruption of current summer programs and faculty reluctance to forego their present schedule, lies in the necessity to accurately predict and equalize student enrollment in each term. Students must be admitted each semester in equivalent numbers. Without this, maximum efficiency is seriously impaired. The study's conclusions were succinct. "As long as these two conditions are not met, the type of program is not significant."[38] Year-round education then becomes, in the administrative aspect, "more expensive and less efficient."[39] Apparently the limitations of the trimester, mathematically interpreted, resemble the problems encountered at the elementary and secondary level in its operation of the staggered four-quarter plan. In each case the burdens of predetermining enrollments are considerable and its dictatorial tone distasteful to administrators.

The Pittsburgh Pattern. The University of Pittsburgh approached its trimester calendar through an extensive three-year development. The year of decision, 1957–58, was comprised of consultation and analysis. All areas of the University were sounded and polled for opinion and counsel. Students protested largely in four categories. They were concerned for the quality of education, suspected extracurricular affairs would be curtailed, held the attitude that they needed a fourth year for "maturity", and logically feared the added expense. In all instances, Pittsburgh seemed able to dispel these apprehensions, except in the matter of funds. (Here it was hoped students would avail themselves of scholarship loans, but the use of these funds in the first trial year was negligible.)

The first year also included a close coordination with the faculty. "A total of 261 out of 353 for whom data were available expressed a willingness to teach three terms,"[40] understanding they "might be allowed one trimester off with full salary every three years."[41] However, "one-fourth of the nine month appointees would not be available,"[42] which meant for administrators, positing full trimester enrollments, that "258 new full-time faculty would be needed."[43] The examining committee did not recognize this "as a disadvantage necessarily."[44] Faculty disapproval of the trimester plan primarily centered around the interference to "research and professional development," consequential intellectual fatigue, and most notably the issue of salary. The 33⅓% increase for 50% additional teaching was not felt to be fully fair. Moreover, academic standards, it was felt, might be unfavorably tilted. Poor articulation with high school schedules was cited. These, and other concerns, needs for increased administrative staffs, more available laboratory space, and so forth, were all digested by the investigating committee and the decision for the trimester was nonetheless effected.

In the end, a trimester plan resembling the Rutgers model was established. The Pittsburgh trimester calls for three terms of 15 weeks, the first term beginning in late August and ending before Christmas, the second running from the New Year into mid-April, and the third term extending from the end of April into early August. Approximately four weeks are set aside for vacations and the necessary housekeeping. Arbitrary assignment of student registration, however, was not attempted, nor were the conventional "summer activities" proscribed. Still, the summer session at Pittsburgh was abruptly toppled into an extremely restricted position. "Under the trimester plan," the Pittsburgh committee announced, "the elementary courses now offered in the summer session would be transferred to the spring trimester, leaving in the summer session those courses needed by public school teachers, graduate students . . . . and summer students from other campuses. It is estimated that such a change in the summer session . . . . would probably cause a 50% reduction in enrollment."[45] The committee later observed "it is probable that the character of the summer session will change,"[46] and suggested that specialization, guest lecturer programs and the like would replace the once regular offering of courses. Whether it will also change into a costly and burdensome appendage remains to be seen, and felt. A second year, 1958–59, was devoted to planning, the development of a priority list, and the elaboration of phase-by-phase procedure. The pilot run was made in 1959–60.

Trimester Variations

Because of its thorough documentation, the Pittsburgh experiment is considered central to discussions of the trimester calendar. Nevertheless other institutions studying its groundbreaking operation are aware of Pittsburgh's particularity, and indeed university officials there have stated the local relativity of their experiment. As opposed to many land-grant state universities, Pittsburgh does not have a large number of varying summer sessions. It serves also an urban population. Other proposals for the trimester calendar at Wayne, Delta, and the Universities of Michigan and Massachusetts follow the Pittsburgh pattern, but with numerous variations.

The Split-Third Term Plan. Most important perhaps of the variations has been the plan developed at the University of Michigan. Termed "the split-third term plan," it "embodies features of both the trimester plan and an expanded summer session plan. . . . Basically (it is) a trimester plan with two 15½ week semesters and a third semester of 15 weeks split into two seven-and-one-half week divisions."[47] Term dates are August-December, January-May, May-June/June-August. It is readily apparent that this system considerably softens the transitional period, provides for careful integration of the summer teaching program, and offers a significant flexibility for the faculty. Simultaneously it eliminates the undesirable feature of the "lame-duck" session.

The significant differences between the Michigan plan and the Pittsburgh trimester lie in the treatment of the summer session. Obviously Michigan's obligations to provide summer service to a wide range of clients, from high school teachers to housewives, is more consuming. Hence their summer session, rather than being flayed, is carefully woven into the fabric of its year-round operation. "The third term would begin in May and end in August. During the third term or spring-summer term, some courses would be offered throughout the entire term, during the first half and during the second one half. This latter portion, which would be given in July and August would meet the needs of the student body which has traditionally enrolled during the summer."[48] Moreover, Michigan appears to be less interested in acceleration than Pittsburgh. "Each student should proceed at the pace best suited to him, which, in the majority of cases, might approximate the present academic calendar."[49]

The 14-Week Trimester. Thad L. Hungate and Earl J. McGrath have proposed a variant trimester three-year degree program with the following characteristics: (1) the academic year would have three terms of 14 weeks each, (2) each student would attend class for nine terms (three years) of 13 weeks each, (3) an extra week would be added to each term for administrative procedures and exams, (4) in each year students and staff would have free periods between terms of three, three, three, and four weeks, (5) every faculty member would be free of institutional obligations one term every three years.

Hungate and McGrath say more students would use this calendar year-round "because the pace is more leisurely than in the 15- or 16-week trimester plan." They make no provisions for abbreviated summer sessions.[50]

Hungate and McGrath believe their trimester calendar can (1) encourage more students of marked ability to accelerate their education, (2) ease the shortage of teachers by making the services of faculty members available for a longer percentage of the calendar year, (3) attract promising young people into college teaching by raising their salaries and giving them triennial sabbaticals, (4) reduce costs of operation and capital outlay, (5) improve the economics of such auxiliary enterprises as dormitories.

All these goals can be reached without any lowering of academic standards or without imposing undue burdens on either faculty members or students, they say in stressing that only such a revision of the academic calendar can "prepare the enterprise of higher education to meet the increased demands which American society will soon place upon it."[51]

The 12-Week Summer Term. It would appear that the Michigan plan, by so muting the relatively abrupt change characterizing the Pittsburgh experiment, and by retaining a short summer term for its peculiar clientele, would be more applicable to the large land-grant university currently operating an extensive and varied summer session. On the other hand, it represents an advance from mere expansion of the summer session. At the University of California year-round operation has been attempted by the integration of its 12-week summer session. Its various campuses have the option of offering either the 12-week summer session as a single unit or dividing it into 6-week segments. Illinois and Wisconsin are testing the 12-week summer term, but Michigan planners noted that this pattern "does not eliminate the lame-duck post-Christmas session,"[52] and added that "it can hardly be said to represent integrated operation. The summer session differs in length, concept, and treatment from the two semesters."[53] Michigan's split-third term plan, then, falls in the middle of current experimentation in year-round operation as a workable compromise.

Whatever the pattern, year-round education represents an end, the inculcation of increased responsibility and seriousness of purpose in the student and the facilitation of his productive entry into society. It also represents a means, the necessary change from the traditional calendar to an accelerated schedule, and a method of increasing the use of the existing plant facility.

THE LONG DEBATE

The problems and merits of year-round education and its accelerative aspects have a long history of discussion and experimentation. The Sheffield Scientific School at Yale University, for example, operated on an accelerated three-year basis from 1847 to 1920. Harvard's President C. W. Eliot proposed a three-year undergraduate program for that institution in 1900 and met with an intransigent Board of Overseers. There is, however, some difference between the debate then and now.

The Yale–Harvard Axis

Although Eliot's pronouncements are dutifully echoed today, his emphasis varied. There was not, at the turn of the century, an unparalleled mass of students bearing down on American campuses, nor was the availability of physical space and the need for efficient institutional operation so insistently acute. It was, on the whole, a more leisurely age, and its approach to problems much less statistical. Early advocates of accelerated education, notably Eliot and later A. L. Lowell, his successor at Harvard, primarily desired earlier admittance. While Eliot did manage to impose a tentative three-year program at Harvard, from 1902 to 1912, it was bitterly fought by a powerful combination of Associated Harvard Clubs and the Board of Overseers. Although punitive extra-tuition charges were levied on those students participating in the program, by 1908 a surprising 37% of 379 graduating A.B.'s had secured their degrees in three years. Eliot's successor, A. L. Lowell, took up the major thesis that the average admission age of 18 years and 10 months was "an extravagant limit."[54] Speaking in 1913, Lowell observed that "men are beginning their careers in life too old, and that the period of education is too long."[55] He went on to assert that "seventeen is a more appropriate age than eighteen to begin the life of college."[56] He touched also on a crucial argument deployed against acceleration. "Much has been said of maturity, but this is the result less of age than of environment and responsibility. Maturity may easily become over-ripe."[57]

Even then sufficient documentation existed to support Lowell's contention. A study of 5,769 students at Harvard from 1902 to 1912 showed that the youngest students "had the best academic records, proportionately graduated more often with honors, and presented fewer disciplinary problems."[58] To this were added corresponding studies with similar findings made at Northwestern, Minnesota, Dartmouth, Columbia, and NYU. The charge of immaturity, however, persisted obstinately. Certainly these early analyses corroborate the current attitude, which only recently has gained public acceptance, that the accelerated student may be socially advanced as well. Drawing from experience with Ford scholars (exceptionally bright high school students accelerated into college), the general conclusion now is that the successful adaptation by these young students "suggested that radical changes in educational procedure may be made without endangering the social or emotional development of students and may even facilitate their growth and adjustment."[59]

James B. Conant, former president of Harvard University, has said: "I am as enthusiastic about the three-year program as I was nearly 50 years ago when, as an undergraduate, I took advantage of it at Harvard."[60]

The three-year study program, then, cannot be seen as a prior failure. In operation at a number of schools, at Johns Hopkins University from 1876 to 1907, and at Clark University from 1902 to 1922, its subsequent demise, as was the case at Harvard, would seem to be due to external pressures rather than failings intrinsic to the system. Clark's accelerated schedule collapsed in 1922 because "students . . . . wanted more time for the usual extracurricular activities,"[61] and because of problems of accreditation, total semester-hours being less than the sum then regarded as necessary by the New York Board of Education. Certainly the self-indulgent attitude of the twenties must be considered; perhaps Clark's student body indeed represented the type of "playpen" undergraduate so severely criticized by Dr. Kirk in 1960.

Only a decade earlier than Clark's dismissal of the three-year program, the National Council of Education, through an appointed investigative committee headed by Dr. J. H. Baker, of the University of Colorado, had stated strongly that "from primary grades to the Ph.D. degree, the period of education is too long."[62] The committee report was filed.

The Pressey Analysis

This curious and general opposition to acceleration was traced at length by Pressey in 1949. "The balance of evidence seemed distinctly in favor of acceleration," he observed, "but prevailing opinion and practice have been against it."[63] In the twenties and thirties, he found, "comparative neglect of means of preventing social maladjustment"[64] coupled with the futility of the Depression significantly impaired any successful exploitation of acceleration. "Acceleration," in the forties and fifties, "has been shunned because of the burdensomeness of the lengthened school year as a method,"[65] plus the difficult social condition of older veterans mingling academically with the younger students. Primarily, then, "each time the main reasons for the failure . . . . have been a fault of method, plus handicapping circumstances."[66]

It should be made clear that in Pressey's thorough analysis of acceleration, year-round calendars are considered as only one method, and not necessarily as a desirable one, toward accelerating students. Other means examined were heavier class loads, credit by examination, and sections for superior students. Pressey's study seemed to regard the matter of acceleration more from the basis of special groups of students than from the thorough-going and involuntaristic accelerative programs envisaged by Kirk and most trimester advocates. "The lengthened school year," Pressey indeed felt, "appears to be unduly burdensome in rigorous professional programs such as medicine and engineering."[67]

Perhaps much of Pressey's data, since it comprises the academic records of wartime and postwar students, might be questioned and presumed aberrant, but certain salient features pertinent to year-round education would seem to be soundly established.

As has been noted earlier, the "saving" of the "productive" years for actual productivity is an emphatic point in all year-round calendar considerations. Calling them "basic neglected concepts," Pressey reinforces the fleeting primacy of the peak years in terms of social contribution. Having made a thorough study of the frequency of illness and death at different ages, and changes with age in strength and quickness,[68] Pressey synthesized the material into charts which clearly showed "the healthiest years appear . . . . to be in the middle twenties," and because of this, "the extension of full-time education far into the twenties would seem . . . . undesirable."[69] To support this, an analysis was made of the age of greatest intellectual alertness and productivity[70] with the finding that there was "a quick mounting to a peak in the early twenties, then a gradual . . . . decline in what has been called mental alertness."[71]

During World War II, a faculty-composed Special Committee on Emergency Educational Policy at The University of Wisconsin, in recommending a 15-week summer session, or third semester, as a solution to wartime manpower needs, took note of its temporary status and declared, "though students are permitted to take three semesters of work a year, they should not be encouraged to do so since for normal conditions and the average student, the practice is educationally unsound."[72] Opposed to this fairly typical view, and the subordinate criticism that accelerated students enter the responsibilities of adult life while still too immature, Dr. Pressey did a survey of length of education as related to age of first notable accomplishment, using entries in *American* and *Current Biography*. Significantly he found that "early beginning and completion of college programs tend to make for success and early accomplishment in adult life."[73] Assuredly such findings are highly relative, and may not be applicable to schools contemplating thorough calendar revision for *all* students, but they do serve to undermine the somewhat perverted image of the typical accelerated student as a neurotically unbalanced *wunderkind*.

The strangeness of the accelerated student, his apartness, has long been known, along with the problems he faces in a society accustomed and geared to the regular academic pattern. "I was admitted to Columbia University," recalls one notable educator, "on the basis of being a high school graduate when I already had a bachelor's degree and master's in math (except for my thesis) for only one reason: I hadn't spent enough years in college."[74] Ultimately, he decided, "the time spent is not necessarily a valid measure of accomplishment on the part of the faculty or of the student."[75] Pressey's conclusions, then, albeit general in nature, may have the specific relevance of acute common sense. Certainly the extensive documentation of the successful social adjustment of Ford scholars would seem to substantiate the view that age and maturity go not necessarily hand in hand.

Wartime Experiences

Perhaps postwar reluctance to year-round education stems from the disappointing wartime acceleration programs. Individual or select-group acceleration has never encountered the severe reaction of involuntary three-year programs, and logically so. But the application of year-round education upon the body of students, average and bright, requires further study. Such imposed programs may anticipate a "time, which may arrive during the next two decades, when only those capable, motivated, and mature students who give reasonable promise of being able to assume responsibility for a major portion of their planning and study, should be encouraged to attend universities."[76] A Stanford report envisaged such a situation: "All students in the university will soon be bright."[77] Naturally, in this hypothetical framework, the accelerated calendar is highly adaptive. But it is unlikely that such a "European" pattern will ever dominate the American scene. So important apprehensions linger. The effects of year-round education on the student, on both his physical and intellectual stamina, have yet to be adequately calculated.

During the war accelerated programs were most inclusive in medicine. In 1943 virtually all medical schools in the U.S. condensed the traditional four years of medical curriculum into three-year programs by eliminating the summer vacation. Although the prime objective—more doctors—was realized, serious complaints from both faculty and students incurred. In the three years before June 30, 1942, 15,535 doctors were graduated. By 1945 the three years had produced 20,662 doctors, an increase of 5,127. Yet because of a shortage of teachers, with all the resultant stress on faculty and students, there was "fairly general agreement that the accelerated program . . . . has been educationally unsound."[78] A variety of reasons were cited: greater superficiality in learning, less tenacity of retention, and a minimum of time for the leisure of contemplation.

This held true as well for engineering schools which also operated three-year programs. It was commonly felt "that a large proportion of students in medicine and engineering looked unfavorably upon the accelerated programs."[79] Polls at Ohio State University during 1944–52 discovered that involuntarily accelerated students looked nostalgically upon the September to June pattern as "normal and natural," and realized their status embodied "apartness" from the regularities of campus life. Most importantly, the work increase was regarded suspiciously by both faculty and students. Some students found it unduly oppressive. Medical faculties were in almost total agreement that the three-year program harassed as well as intensified student progress. Of course, trimesters presumably would place the entire campus on the year-round schedule, thus eliminating the alienation of the accelerated student, but the handicapping problem of work load, as medical and engineering students found it, remains to be solved.

The situation with individual accelerated students, voluntarily enrolled in three-year programs, was radically different. On the average, they led successful and balanced collegiate careers. Time studies at Ohio State University, comparing the regular with the accelerated student, found that in the use of time there was "no significant difference between non-accelerated and accelerated students."[80] Pressey's evaluation of acceleration, then, tends to disparage involuntary lengthenings of the school year, appropos the accelerated medical schools, in favor of more direct and specific means of acceleration in relation to individual students. The merits of trimesters and other calendar revisions, it seems to be inferred, cannot be effectively assessed in their value to students. Because of the incalculable diversity of intelligence and application within students as a group, their present capability to undertake intensified programs cannot be predicted. Significantly, considering the unfavorable wartime experience with acceleration, the University of Pittsburgh found difficulties in accreditation and licensure with the very schools, engineering and medicine, that were accelerated during the War.

The history of year-round education is thus chameleon-like. Viewed alternately as a temporary corrective measure and as a basic reform, it has become in the postwar years the synthesis of both; its type of acceleration seen both as a means and an end. While it is now in many quarters agreed that the educational process can and should be intensified, and that the utilization of a year-round calendar under optimum conditions can result in comparative economies, that the efficiency of accelerated operation necessarily corresponds with quality of education is still in contention. The student and the professor have occupied in the long debate the critical position. In the delicate requirements of the four-quarter or the trimester, they remain unknown ingredients.

THE BONES OF CONTENTION

The Student

In an earlier time, when the university was a stumbling child but a few steps removed from the darkness of the Dark Ages, students were an obstreperous and powerful social cadre quite unlike their meek modern counterparts. An administration unto themselves, they hired and fired their professors, dealt with the alien townsmen, and when civic relations soured merely moved their school to another and more congenial community. It was only later that faculties subjected them to discipline, perhaps because the proud unbowed student himself became the teacher and would not be harried. From that date, however, the student rather than being a self-determining creature became an object of solicitude and dictation.

In the broad sense, the student must now take what he can get. His education is pre-arranged. His voice in the operation of his university, while he is an attending student, is at best a squeak.

What Price Acceleration? A calendar change to year-round education, however tentative, has significant bearing on the student. It implies finally a quickened tempo, a more strenuous pattern of learning for him. Inevitably, for many students, it means the loss of his traditional summer of rest and recreation. The historic resistance to educational acceleration centers around student fatigue, plainly his "studying too hard." It has repeated the homily that a hot July afternoon, when the fish are biting and the girls waiting to be wooed, is incompatible with concentration on an Anglo-Saxon verse form or a complicated theorem. In this it has made no distinction between the ten-year-old and the young man of eighteen. It's just too hot in summer. Eleven months of school is excessive. Proponents of acceleration, on the other hand, point to an impressive body of documentation clearly showing that a stepped-up pace and summer study are in no way detrimental to the student.

The Committee on Higher Education in New York State in 1960 expressed the conviction that the three-year pattern should be the "standard plan" for all students except those who must work their way through college.[81] But just how such a revolution in American habits is to be brought about, Mr. Heald and his colleagues did not specify.

Columbia College (South Carolina) reports that the possibility of year-round attendance increases the longer a student has been in residence, and that its newly established and upgraded term is proving to be a better drawing card than the previously scheduled summer sessions.[82]

President Grayson Kirk of Columbia University has said:

"Physicians and psychiatrists assure me normal youngsters can take three terms in stride. During World War II many students were on a 48-week schedule, and the level of performance never was higher. . . . The trimester plan involves no sacrifice of academic elements or undergraduate tribal customs. There may even be more participation in extracurricular activities with students' attention focused on the campus 45 weeks a year. Sports can continue on the present basis by dropping the freshman eligibility rule, as it was during the War."[83]

When the Committee on Higher Education in New York State (the Heald Committee) recommended the year-round calendar in 1960, upstate New York newspapers pointed out that:

"The change to year-round schooling makes sense for all students except those who utilize the summer months to earn part of the costs of going to college. . . . It will cost the student more during the three years but he will be ahead of the game. He will be able to take his first job earlier—have money coming in at least a year ahead of time.[84]

Until the advent of Pittsburgh's adoption of the trimester plan, there were no large scale experiments with year-round education in the postwar years. Schools that operated accelerated three-year programs realized successfully their temporary manpower goals and reverted to the traditional nine-month calendar when the emergency receded. One effect of this experience has been a type of double-vision on the part of educators in regarding year-round operation. Pressey, as has been seen, tended to look upon the lengthened school year as the poorest method of acceleration. The careful harboring of lingering doubts may be seen in his conclusion to an Ohio State study of the class of 1942–43 in which 33% of the graduating class had earned their degrees in three years. "The evidence is that acceleration 'the hard way'—primarily by going to school four quarters instead of three—has worked reasonably well," Pressey observed. "But surely there must be less clumsy methods for acceleration."[85] While undoubtedly the unhappy causes of wartime acceleration, the shortage of teachers, and the generally hectic pace of living then were large factors in the negative reaction to acceleration, the attitude has been carried forward generally by faculties. "It is our opinion," a Michigan calendar committee reported, "that faculty members generally react negatively to any proposals for year-round operation. . . . Many of us remember with dismay the year-round operation in the service programs during World War II, and hope we will never have to participate in anything like that again!"[86]

Still, the winds of change are blowing. It will be recalled that medical schools almost unanimously disapproved of year-round programs for their students, and were eager to change back to the prewar calendar when the war was over. It was felt then that medical students were oppressed by continuous attendance and that faculties also felt the burden of constant stress. Students in the critical professional schools considered their education hurried and shallow. Overwork was the key word. Yet at Columbia Medical School a year-round calendar has been established with stated aims directly contradictory to the wartime experience. The year-round term of study condenses five calendar years into four, leaving students one month a year of vacation. Dean Rappleye reported that the plan "has given the student a real sense of responsibility."[87] Within the continuous four-year program, it is felt, the student's flexibility of choice is increased. Primarily, "the whole undergraduate medical course must be looked upon as a unit, not as a series of independent . . . . compartments."[88] These two points reflect, of course, basic principles in current year-round calendar studies. Where "overwork" was once the dominant characteristic of year-round education, 'flexibility' has replaced it. Dean Rappleye believes the integrated year-round program will not only provide more comprehensive training but an increased availability of courses and time to allow the student particular concentrations in certain fields while yet an undergraduate.

Acceleration is a topic that has been thoroughly researched and evaluated, and it is difficult to find a derogatory analysis. In the main, however, such studies have dealt with superior students, with early entrants, students using the various means of acceleration—credit by examination and special courses. Year-round education, as has been noted, is only one of the accelerative means. The applicability, then, of past experiments and studies, because they focused primarily on elite fractions of the student body, is questionable. Colleges and universities contemplating year-round calendars must certainly hope that more than a small number of its attending students will use the added term. Still, there are interesting aspects to these studies of acceleration that may shed some light, however speculative, on the role of students, average and bright, in year-round programs. One analysis of accelerants at Clark University found that while the young entrants were not, on the average, "inferior to the older ones in actual achievement on subjects dealing with economics, sociological and philosophical problems . . . . that one-third of the young entrants stated that they felt a lack of experience necessary for the study and discussion of such questions."[89] Underlying this observation is the shibboleth of immaturity, the lack of "life" experience which enables a student a more meaningful and correlated pursuit "of such questions." On the other hand, a comparable study found that the accelerant "participates to a considerable extent in extracurricular affairs . . . . and he continues his education fully as far as the student who is two years older."[90] The question of maturity, then, remains highly relative, with the findings of experiments fluctuating considerably. In general it would appear that accelerated students are not socially or emotionally impeded, but the criteria, extracurricular participation, offices held and the like, are obviously loosely broad for such a determination.

Perhaps the most applicable study for the purposes of this monograph was carried out in 1946, pairing sixty-seven undergraduate women who graduated in three years or less, going four quarters, with a sister group who took the regular four years. A grade comparison found that "completion of a college program in three years thus appears not to have seriously affected scholarship. . . ."[91] A detailed analysis was made as to the social and physical effect of year-round education on the women. It was found again that "in short, the data indicates saving of an academic year of time with, for the most part, no lowering of scholarship or impairment of health and relatively little handicap as to social and recreational life."[92]

Another study attempting to determine if immaturity was a hampering effect of acceleration was done on three graduating classes, 1926–27, 1927–28, and 1933–34, in periods of both prosperity and depression. The accelerants' records of achievement were compared with those of similar students who had graduated at 22. The means of acceleration was early admission. The study's concluding remarks asked, "Did they graduate too young? Were they immature? The answer is an emphatic negative. These younger graduates outdid their elders in securing advanced degrees . . . . a greater number of them secured teaching positions . . . . throughout the record of the younger graduates is as good as, or better than, that of the older."[93]

More recently, Gustav and Crosman have asked the question whether or not younger-than-standard students matched up to their older colleagues. Their data tell us that a fairly large proportion of the younger students at Washington Square College had difficulty in college which, perhaps, more careful admissions screening might have predicted. On the other hand, "the fact that more than half had satisfactory records, and at the very high levels they matched the total enrollment, would seem to indicate that youthfulness, *per se,* should not be a bar to acceleration at lower school levels and to college admission. Indeed, a generalization might be drawn that, since brighter students can handle such acceleration, schools ought to permit it."[94]

A study at the University of Buffalo comparing accelerants with "equally able and equally well-prepared students who spent four years at the university and received all their credits by regular instruction,"[95] was done with the aim of determining social and academic effects of acceleration. Sixty-nine of the accelerated group "obtained bachelors' degrees in three years or less."[96] Of these 32 attended school year-round, utilizing Buffalo's summer program. Again the findings significantly established that "academic achievements do not decrease."[97] Between the two groups there was no important scholastic difference. Also accelerants proved to be equally as active in social participation. In fact, so matched were the performances of the two groups that only one important factor distinguishes them. The accelerants accomplished as much and as well in three years as did their peers in four years. What is immediately suggested by the record of the accelerants is that the four-year student needlessly wasted a year.

The cry, then, for the fourth year, for the four summer rest periods as being necessary to the emotional development of the student begins to soften. Beyond a general feeling that this is so, and an occasional neurotic bookworm to use as case in point, there is no concrete evidence to support the contention. To the contrary, as has been seen, three-year programs, early matriculation, and summer study have aided and abetted students in their later careers.

Perhaps, after all, the primary problems a student faces undertaking the acceleration of year-round study are practical ones, issues important enough but not necessarily related to the task of learning. An Ohio State study of 64 "problem" students ("the misfits of academic society—the students most apt to be bothered by the additional strain of continuous attendance"[98]) compared the 28 who were in school the year-round with the 36 who were absent during the summer session. The study indicated "that those who chose voluntarily to attend year-round tend to be somewhat more intelligent than those who do not attend during the summer."[99] Also, "other evidence indicates that such voluntary attenders tend to be more sensitive to seeking solutions to their problems."[100] These students, asked to rank year-round attendance among 12 other sources of student problems, placed it in the relatively lesser important ninth position. Moreover, a "thorough acquaintance with the students does not uncover many instances of bad effects of personality growth from year-round attendance."[101] Indeed the chief disadvantages of continuous study seemed to be on practical matters. "On the whole, the main drawbacks to year-round attendance seems to be difficulties in finance and loss of work experience."[102]

Year-round education, then, in relation to the student has been studied at both ends of the student spectrum and its effects evaluated on the superior and the problem student. In both instances this type of acceleration was seen as beneficial. Practical considerations, however, remain.

Dollars and Sense. The University of Pittsburgh estimated that the student participating fully in the trimester program would increase his expense some 50%. Presuming that his early matriculation, and hence his continuous study, remains the prime objective of such a calendar change, the facts of finance become paramount. A survey at Michigan in 1956 "showed that 28% of the University's students were entirely self-supporting, and that 36% were partially self-supporting. This indicates that 64% were supporting themselves to some degree."[103] Over half, then, of this large state university's student body were actively, personally investing in their education, and presumably, because of incentive, constituted the most likely enrollment for continuous study. It is also likely that they would be the least able to afford the additional expenditure and loss of summer income. A similar situation exists at The University of Wisconsin where during 1961 "some 65 per cent of the undergraduate students had applied savings, and half of these had savings of approximately $346 or more; this means that for at least 4,500 undergraduates (32%) summer school attendance would have represented a serious loss in income."[104]

The solution to this, of course, lies in the greater utilization of educational loans and availability of scholarship awards. The same Wisconsin study mentioned above revealed "a significant number of UW undergraduate students for whom summer study would seem to have been economically feasible, given modest scholarships and/or loans."[105] This alternative, however, is not easily come by. There has been historic reluctance on the part of the students to borrow on their education, and the additional appropriations for financial grants may not readily be forthcoming. Tentative reports on Pittsburgh's trimester student indicate the importance of finance. Students interested in the three-year program were generally from higher socio-economic backgrounds, and thus were not personally liable for their educational costs. "Of the students not planning to enroll in the third semester, 86% planned to work. . . ."[106] Also, students planning to attend professional or graduate schools are more likely to enroll in the three-year plan. "The study also reveals no significant differences between two-term and three-term attendance in credits carried or in credits of failure."[107] The inference drawn from this is that the third term is being used primarily as a means of acceleration.

A University of Michigan calendar report, however, viewed the problem of finance differently, regarding year-round education more as a help than a hindrance. "In many areas, the fall, winter or spring present better opportunities for student employment than does the summer. Certainly, by diverting some of the present student labor supply from summer to the other seasons, the total opportunity for student employment will be increased."[108] This, however, can be strongly argued in other areas that are less industrialized, where much of the student employment is in summer work.

A person who accelerates his college program by one year makes up for loss of interim income by entering his field of work a year earlier at the going age. This fact leads many educators to encourage "educational" borrowing. It would seem, in essence, that the money problem is not insurmountable. Even where a complicated machinery of financial assistance does not exist, the earnest student, as Dr. Kirk intimated in his *Saturday Evening Post* article, makes his way.

Everybody Talks About the Weather. Unfortunately there have been no extensive experiments studying the effects of warm weather upon student performance. In the early part of this century, Ellsworth Huntingdon, a climatologist, made a comprehensive evaluation of performance in civil service examinations in Massachusetts and New York, the grades of West Point and Annapolis students, and the relative number of amendments to patent applications. These he charted on graphs in relation to the seasons. He found that "all have maxima in spring and fall, with minima in summer and winter. The spring maximum is systematically higher or more prolonged than the autumn maximum, whereas the summer minimum tends to be lower than that of winter."[109] On these graphs, in each case, summer performance sagged impressively. The study, however, was compiled long before the advent of air conditioning. It directly contradicts, moreover, the reports of summer study compiled in Newark, Aliquippa, and Ambridge. Pragmatically Huntingdon's findings do not hold up when contrasted with the successful operation of the country's flourishing summer sessions. A University of Minnesota study comparing learning achievement of summer session students who were taught by a "concentrated" method with achievement of regular quarter students who were taught by the "distributed" method showed "no significant difference in achievement between summer term and regular academic quarter students as measured by the usual examination."[110]

In detail the Minnesota study examined student performance in three courses taught both in the regular quarter and in the summer term. "Common to all three were the characteristics that summer and regular quarter sections were taught by the same instructor, textbooks were the same, and course examinations were identical or comparable. A fourth characteristic, not as consistently reflected in each set of courses, was that summer term students were comparable to regular quarter students."[111] From this rigidly controlled assessment, and drawing from earlier like experiments, the study concluded "the overwhelming consensus of the findings is that where the material to be learned is meaningful, in contrast to nonsense syllables, for example, the distribution of learning time is not a critical variable."[112] More specifically, "there is no difference in learning achievement as reflected in course examinations, between summer term sections and regular quarter sections of the same course."[113]

To a degree, the Armed Forces foreign language programs operated during the War verify the Minnesota findings. They are valuable also in that their compressed periods of study did not evidently result in any serious psychological strains. "In April, 1943, 15,000 trainees were under this system (Army Specialized Training Program (ASTP).) The course, in general, consisted of three consecutive trimesters of 12 weeks each, with one week's vacation between trimesters for relaxation and reclassification." Moreover, "the actual number of instructional hours in the intensive program exceeded by far the time spent in class under the traditional system. For the intensive program of nine months or about thirty-six weeks with 17 hours per week yielded a total of 612 instructional hours as compared with 300 hours in the traditional language study covering two or three years of college."[114] P. F. Angiolillo, in reviewing that formidable program, reported that "most of the trainees displayed greater enthusiasm than is seen in regular classes."[115]

The academic achievement of these soldier-students, moreover, was comparable to language levels attained by regular students, and in some instances impressively higher. Speaking of the ASTP program operated at The University of Wisconsin during the War, Rehder and Twaddell noted that "a reading knowledge test . . . showed that at the end of the thirty-third week all trainees were at a stage of competence corresponding to "Pass" or better on the basis of national six-semester norms."[116] Sidney J. French, a coordinator in the military school system, remarked, "This work has shown me that prewar liberal-arts-college education was a leisurely way of killing four good years in a young man's life."[117] We are back, then, to a theme struck earlier in this chapter, by men like C. W. Eliot, A. L. Lowell, and Grayson Kirk. The properly motivated student is capable of far greater challenges and work than is now required of him.

The problems of year-round education for the student thus appear to be external, those of finance and work experience. Experiments with three-year programs have shown no appreciable immaturity in students, no lessening in the depth of knowledge, and no impairment of mental and physical health. The negative effects of summer study have been seen as non-existent.

The Teacher

Faculty reactions to year-round education are cautious and mixed. Because of the variety of proposals and their various significances to teachers in terms of time and pay, it is difficult to generalize a consistent attitude or opinion. To speak of the problems of the teacher in year-round programs is also a topic primarily bound to local circumstances. At the University of Pittsburgh, when the faculty was polled for their opinion of the trimester plan, "a total of 261 out of 353 for whom data were available expressed a willingness to teach three terms" with the qualification that they be "allowed one trimester off with full salary every three years."[118] Michigan, on the other hand, found in a similar poll that "faculty members generally react negatively to any proposals for year-round operation."[119] In both institutions, however, such programs are now either in effect or scheduled for operation. At both schools calendar committees included faculty representatives, and in each case their participation was instrumental in devising the final plan. If, as David McKenna has suggested in his article, "The Academic Calendar in Transition," faculties have not played a significant part in either the initiation or execution of calendar reforms, they have had considerable voice and weight in determining the kind of adjusted program under which they would be working. Obviously any institution imposing a disagreeable year-round plan upon its faculty places both its status and standards in jeopardy.

It has been sufficiently established that teachers on the whole regarded the accelerated programs of the Second World War with extreme distaste. The charges of intellectual fatigue, of subsequent shoddy teaching, of scarce time for professional development, particularly among engineering and medical faculties, undoubtedly had merit at that time. Whether, under current programs and at the present time, they continue to have substance is the point to be determined.

It would appear that the majority of year-round programs presently under consideration and implementation are skillfully drawn to leave the teacher a reasonable degree of flexibility. In some cases, as with Michigan's split third-term plan, it is argued that professional development is enhanced. Pittsburgh also makes this claim. The nine-month appointee "actually has a two months longer period for continued study."[120] Then, too, by the availability of increased teaching time, members of faculties are provided the opportunity of augmenting their income, although frequently at rates below the regular-year norms. Michigan has pointed out that teaching the summer term has the advantage of taking the customary vacation in either winter or spring when European universities and educational facilities are in operation. Year-round education, then, should not be automatically linked to year-round teaching. Both at Pittsburgh and Michigan, the annual term of appointment is left optional. In its most severe expression, a teacher working all three terms or four quarters would still have a month of vacation and one full-length term every two or three years in which to recuperate or pursue private study. Even at that, many schools, notably Michigan, in their systems of year-round operation, merely carry over and expand the possibilities now available to the teacher under the traditional calendar. Whether stress and a lower calibre of performance will evidence itself in teachers working three consecutive terms remains to be seen and documented.

Certainly at perhaps the more harassed pace of the elementary and secondary teacher, year-round education has not proved detrimental. The Brinkerhoff analysis of Newark's all-year schools failed to find any impairment of health or mental attitude in its participating teachers. The Vanderslice study of Aliquippa's quarter program came to similar conclusions, noting additionally that teacher applications to Aliquippa's all-year school increased with its implementation. While there have been notable dissensions, based primarily on the theory that teachers require the summer for recuperation, experience has held the contrary.

Undeniably the attraction of 12-month employment to the generally low-salaried primary and high school teacher is strong. In certain communities year-round education has come, in fact, to focus particularly on the teacher. One summer program for professional personnel, based on the year-round utilization facilities, works on a five-year cycle. Three summers of the five, the teacher works on a curriculum and teaches summer courses, one summer she studies for academic improvement, and in the fifth she is allowed leave. A personal communication with one teacher under the program at Glencoe, Illinois, yielded an enthusiastic and positive response. In Rochester and Lexington teacher reaction to this plan has been overwhelmingly favorable. While assuredly this is an optimal environment for the teacher, it must be remembered that the Newark all-year school, established in depressed areas, also encountered no appreciable recalcitrance with its faculty.

On the issue of calendar change, one Pittsburgh administrator observed that "in general, the faculty seems strongly to favor the status quo,"[121] perhaps illustrating in that remark a nebulous yet essential factor in faculty opposition to year-round programs. The traditionalism of faculties is storied, and while there may be no statistics to prevail, their resentment toward any suspected erosion of their privileges is equally as known and felt. It has been said that one main privilege, adequate time for research and professional improvement, appears to be protected under the Pittsburgh trimester and ensured by the Michigan plan, although in Pittsburgh's first year of operation "details for budgeting faculty time for research, teaching sabbaticals, and vacations have not in every case been specifically determined."[122] At a 1961 conference at the University of Pittsburgh, "a representative of the American Council on Education reported the accumulating evidence that faculty do not actually do the quantity of research they are supposedly doing."[123] Whether this is a crystallized opinion in the minds of administrators, and thus wordlessly calculated by them, is unknown. At Pittsburgh, while "it was admitted . . . that the faculty . . . did seem 'hurried' the first term on the trimester and passed this feeling of 'rushing along' to their students,"[124] it was felt this was a natural phase in the transitional period. Generally, "the attitude of the faculty to the trimester has shown some change for the better and the attitude of new faculty is extremely favorable."[125] The Michigan calendar report stated the opinion that its split third-term would enhance its recruiting stance.

If not explicitly stated, nevertheless, it is a safely deducible guess that many faculties might see in calendar changes an administrative encroachment on hitherto exclusive departmental and divisional provinces; curriculum, for example. "An incidental effect," a Pittsburgh report stated, "of upsetting routine practices in order to introduce the new calendar has been the encouragement of faculties to rethink their entire programs in terms of basic objectives and in terms of student learning experience. . . ."[126]

How real such a division or contest is, once again, varies from school to school. As long as assignments in year-round operation are kept voluntary, largely the policy of individual departments, such a development is unlikely. With a shortage of teachers, however, and an operational commitment to year-round utilization of facilities, the possibility of regimentation remains open. Pittsburgh's reply, "more faculty must be found so that existing faculty is not overworked,"[127] under the future strain of burgeoning enrollments and a hypothetical lack of available faculty, could echo glibly.

Ironically, the very popularity of year-round education, i.e., employment, with teachers poses a certain difficulty. The possibility of younger teachers exhausting themselves intellectually by undertaking continuous teaching assignments, with the design of improving their financial condition, has been discussed at length. For the present, Pittsburgh has referred the problem to the chairmen of individual departments. Undoubtedly policy at schools on the year-round basis is inevitably to be effected, establishing regulatory patterns for length of teaching terms.

In any decision, it must be remembered that while most university professors are ostensibly paid to do one job, the worth of their services is evaluated on the basis of how well they do another. "The work assignment for which the vast majority of professors are paid is teaching. . . . When they are evaluated, however, either as candidates for a vacant position, or as candidates for promotion, the evaluation is made principally in terms of their research contributions to their disciplines."[128]

Faculty members need free time, broadening experiences, research leaves, study opportunities. This can be a problem; the fact that it doesn't seem to be at institutions with the longest year-round experience, such as Baylor, North Carolina, and George Peabody, testifies to the care with which faculty members can be rotated and given sabbaticals and research opportunities. The colleges and universities mentioned desire to run the plant year-round, not the faculty.[129]

The Administration

David McKenna has suggested that the rationale of year-round calendars largely is based on the need to enlarge the capacity of schools to serve more students, and secondarily to increase the efficiency of operation and to improve academic quality. Within this framework two kinds of motivation are seen as causes of calendar change. One, termed external, cites the need to intensify education to fulfill manpower needs and satisfy the oncoming swell of enrollments. The other, called internal, is perhaps more lively in the minds of trustees and administrators. It encompasses a desire to improve the image of the institution as efficient and full-time in hopes of receiving increased financial support, the opportunity to enhance the competitive position of the school in attracting and preserving faculty with the leverage of higher salaries, and the possible position of being able to facilitate other changes, curriculum revision and administration reorganization, through the machinery of calendar reform. These internal motives, where and when they exist to a considerable degree, cause conflict "because they seem to imply an over-concern with the demand for increasing the efficiency of the institution at the expense of the educational purpose."[130] In his article, McKenna groups concern for year-round education around three images: the "numbers" image of the public, concerned with the availability of higher education for their children; the "efficiency" image of the administration; and the "quality" image of faculties. Around each of these "interests" suspicion of the other sector's motives arises and leads to controversy. "The complete reappraisal of the curriculum," a University of Pittsburgh report noted, "with the resulting pruning of courses was one of the really outstanding by-products of the new program."[131] The University of Michigan expressly stated "in academic circles 'efficiency' is not necessarily a desirable goal, since many of its connotations are pejorative—a reduction in personal relationship, a larger degree of regimentation, and an ultimate lowering of standards."[132] Whether efficiency is necessarily at cross-purpose with these qualities could perhaps be debated.

McKenna asserts that the main operational problem confronting administrations in the change to year-round operation is "the inability of colleges and universities to equalize and predict student enrollment either by attraction or regulation."[133] This factor is the determining premise in the influential Easton analysis of operating schedules on year-round basis. This evaluation studied, mathematically, 12 systems, one the traditional semester calendar and the other 11 year-round programs. Dispensing with four-quarter plans, the study found the trimester provided "as low a cost index and as high use factors as any schedule considered."[134] The optimal trimester plan admitted three times each year an entering class of equivalent size. The normal matriculation period added to from 3 to 3⅔ years. The schedule called for three 16-week terms with classes rotating, in school two terms, out one. The program, however, demands a strenuous administrative effort in order to achieve maximum efficiency. "To realize maximum benefit in cost reduction, faculties would have to serve for 48 weeks per year."[135] Also involved is the almost total elimination of the diversified summer programs, the arbitrary determination of interspersed vacation periods and the requirement both to space and delay student enrollments. A second trimester schedule which calls for continuous attendance of the student throughout the three 16-week terms, and which admits only once, also requires the formidable administrative apparatus. Without full application of the criteria, year-round education, from the engineering standpoint, becomes "more expensive and less efficient."[136] As has been seen, no institution of higher learning, in the pure pursuit of that efficiency, has followed Easton's operational dicta strictly. At Pittsburgh "rather than forcing conformity of participation, the university permitted both the faculty and students to choose terms in which they would enroll and teach."[137] Whereas at the University of Michigan, "the Committee agreed . . . year-round operation must not imply year-round teaching or even year-round attendance."[138] Obviously administrations, by this judicious ministration to faculty and students, impose a handicap upon themselves. According to the Easton analysis, the lack of discipline in registering equal admissions results in inefficiency and increased costs. Still, programs of year-round operation have been carried forward and executed.

Michigan's economic rationale notes that "it is reasonable to expect that year-round operation will eventually result in more economical operation per student taught—although one more expensive *in toto* because more students are being taught. . . . Although direct instructional costs may be expected to increase proportionately to the increase in the function of the university, supporting instructional costs for physical facilities, administration and services will increase in lower ratio. Since these latter costs amount to forty per cent of the total instructional cost, an overall reduction in unit cost of operating the university should be feasible without reducing the economic status or working conditions of the faculty."[139]

Pittsburgh's initial experience has been charted. A 1960 review of its first year of the trimester reported that "overhead costs have been allocated to the two regular trimesters and the summer sessions for purposes of analysis. Using this technique, the Spring term shows a favorable cost-income relationship for the first year of operation. Our original enrollment estimates of 1,000 full-time student equivalents was exceeded by nearly 150% when enrollments reached 2,493 full-time student equivalents. This extremely favorable enrollment trend and the high number of 12-month people employed in the University made the costs much more reasonable."[140]

Hungate and McGrath estimate their trimester plan would reduce staff requirements by 17%, would reduce per-student credit hour costs by 6%, and would reduce capital expenditure by 25%, meanwhile raising the average professor's salary by 21%; but they make clear they are assuming that "a large majority" of students will be in continuous attendance in the three-year degree program.

Without balanced attendance throughout the year, they admit "the costs associated with full-year operation are more than likely to affect the advantages."[141]

Planning the year-round calendar must first crystallize as a decision, and logically, at high administrative levels. The steps have previously been elaborated, with Pittsburgh as an illustration. There are three phases: decision, planning, and implementation. Except for planning, which involves coordination with faculty, student groups, and other sectors, these steps are largely handled by the administration. Implementation at the University of Pittsburgh entailed an outline of eighty major tasks. Their intricacy is only summarily covered in the following description. "These tasks covered every phase of university life and organization including, for example, review of courses, gearing registration to the new calendar, developing policy papers on faculty pay and appointments, reorganizing student activities, and making budget estimates. Every aspect of the transition had to be carefully timed in relation to every other aspect."[142] In effect, a thorough transformation is made. Michigan's split third term plan, however, envisages a smoother, less disruptive change to year-round operation. Nevertheless, at Pittsburgh all schools and divisions, except law, felt they could adapt. A number of divisions, liberal arts among them, served notice they would gear specifically for the purpose of accelerating students. This has not been the major intent at Michigan.

Perhaps, though on a lesser scale, it is the pre-vision of this administrative complexity that intimidates administrators at all levels. Two polls, one in 1951 and a second in 1955, run by the magazine, *The Nations Schools,* reported the position of superintendents almost entirely closed to year-round school proposals. Administration, the difficulty of controlling enrollments, and increased costs, were the main reasons listed for the negative response. The Vanderslice review of Aliquippa's four quarter plan, however, reported considerable economies by their better use of existing school facilities. A Newark study showed that it cost Newark in the period, 1913 to 1923, $561.89 for the all-year school to graduate one student and $800 for the ten-month school. The author of the study, a Newark administrator, favored the all-year program even though "it is more complicated to operate and involves greater administrative skill."[143]

It is difficult to evaluate the role and problems of school administrators in the dynamics of calendar change, since local circumstances will shape them. What will function smoothly and economically at Newark and for the University of Pittsburgh may not necessarily apply for other cities and colleges. It is safe to presume, however, that year-round operation involves a more complicated call for increased workloads. It does not, apparently, necessarily mean a multiplication of persons and duties needed for effective administration. At the relatively large University of Pittsburgh, inaugurating their complex calendar change, "the administrative budget for the third term was increased only $15,000 which was used to hire additional clerks for the registration office."[144]

THE UPSHOT

Just as the traditional academic calendar was the product of one political economy, so the year-round university has as its principal godfather modern social pressures. Educators from Eliot to Kirk have viewed as a waste, to both society and the individual, the leisurely, sporadic pace of higher education, and they have recommended the accelerated calendar as a solution. Legislators and trustees have seized on the same device as a means of cutting down on costly classroom construction in the face of explosive enrollments.

Theoretically it is true that any type of year-round calendar will get students through college faster at less per-capita cost, but in order for this to happen without a significant decline in quality of education, certain conditions must be met. At least two of these conditions represent very big "ifs."

First, student enrollment must be approximately equal in each term, either trimester or quarter; otherwise, operational and capital savings fail to materialize. The private college conceivably could arrange such a stable enrollment by endowing its registrar with Gestapo-like powers; but in the public institution, charged with meeting the kaleidoscopic needs and wants of thousands of individual citizens, it will be extremely difficult to predict, much less arrange, balanced registrations. If and when public bodies dictate that adherence to arbitrary schedules must be the price of attending a state institution, then the year-round calendar becomes feasible; until then, the campus fiscal officer will still have to house peak loads in fall and take what he gets in summer.

The second condition is even more critical, that of making peace with the faculty. If salary schedules under an all-year calendar reflect added pay for added work on the basis of present formulae, there will be no practical problem. But if legislators and trustees expect professors to teach more for comparatively less money, they must also be prepared to accept a steady deterioration in the quality of the faculty and its productive scholarship. Indeed we can envisage a not-too-distant time when a professor shortage could become much more pressing—and much harder to surmount—than the current classroom shortage. This is the Achilles heel of the year-round calendar. Second-rate institutions need not fear it so much as distinguished universities.

When we enter into a consideration of the year-round university, then, we are dealing not only with balance sheets but with profound human tides and stresses that come to focus on faculty-student relationships.

THE SITUATION TODAY

The University of Pittsburgh started the ball rolling toward year-round operation when it adopted the so-called trimester plan in 1959. Other colleges have recently adopted a four-quarter plan like that of the University of Denver. Some universities, while adhering to the traditional two semesters, have added a 12-week summer term. The year-round calendar debate has flourished particularly in tax-supported institutions, which are under pressure to demonstrate to state legislatures that they are making efficient use of their faculties. Florida in 1961 became the first state to require by statute that its university system operate on a year-round basis. New York is launching experimental all-year programs at three state institutions. The Universities of California, Michigan, and Illinois are soul-searching toward expanded summer operations. In Pennsylvania the year-round study plan appears particularly appealing to medical students.

Interest in the extended academic calendar is not limited to the large tax-supported universities, however.[145] Various small colleges are experimenting with new patterns, prodded, perhaps, by the fact that such massive educational foundations as Ford and Carnegie seem currently to be enamored by the flexible thinking that calendar juggling suggests.

The calendar debate has not always been marked by a careful assessment of the effects of a new schedule on a university's stock in trade—students and professors. At the University of Illinois, it has. While a faculty committee there has set as the institution's goal a three-term plan, it has stipulated that no changes should be made until "certain conditions precedent to successful operation of a more intensive program" are fully met.

So critical do these "precedent conditions" seem that they are listed here:

1. Development of a system of registration which will reduce materially the time now spent on this activity.

2. Assurance given to the faculty that any change will not result in reduced remuneration or worsened conditions of employment.

3. A full third term should not be inserted into the calendar until sufficient funds are available to pay for it at the current level of operations.

4. The growth toward a full third term should be gradual and flexible.

5. The shift to three-term operations should be preceded by the widest possible faculty and administrative discussion.

6. The university should establish a pilot project in year-round operation by admitting for the second term, say, two thousand students who might have been denied admission in the first term due to lack of facilities. A third full term could then be developed.[146]

Whether the year-round schedule will become the standard in higher education depends, in the final analysis, on whether enough students and teachers are willing to spend their summers on campus. For maximum economy, the numbers admitted at the beginning of each term must be roughly the same. Trimester and four-quarter schedules are still too new to make it safe to say whether this will be the case. However, signs now point to a steady increase in summer registration at colleges and universities which offer a full schedule of courses in that term, says Editorial Research Reports.[147]

There is plenty of room for expansion. The size of the summer session at American universities tends to run 40 to 50 per cent the size of its academic year counterpart. While the summer faculty is much the same as that of the academic year with respect to rank and degree, comparative salary distributions show that higher ranking faculty tend to earn less in summer because of ceilings of one kind or another. While there is often heard the comment that the summer term involves too concentrated a period of work, there is no statistical evidence that summer learning is any less efficient or effective than learning during the so-called regular year.[148]

If greater utilization of this untapped resource is to be achieved in adequately caring for increasing enrollments, while at the same time strengthening and carrying forward research and service obligations, our colleges and universities will need the understanding and support of legislatures, boards of control, faculties, students, parents, public school officials, and citizens in general.[149]

The summer term is undoubtedly emerging as a significant device through which each college and university can move to attain its objectives. For many, this presages a summer enterprise "as broad as human endeavor and as high as human aspirations."

IV

Problems and Prospects

WHILE THE PATTERNS of all-year education may take many forms, we have seen that as a common denominator they entail virtually continuous operation of the school plant through various devices for employing faculty and for requireing or attracting student attendance around the calendar.

Such a change in academic routine, though seemingly simple, actually represents a distinct wrench to long-established practices sanctified by professional tradition and public acceptance. What is responsible for this upheaval?

THE LONG VIEW

Psychiatrists tell us the line between affection and aggression is a thin one. In the lines of a popular song, "You always hurt the one you love." It has frequently been the fate of our educational system to represent corroborating evidence. Seemingly, nothing is so characteristic of the American idea as a profound faith in the efficacy of education. Yet our schools and colleges become at times the butt of mass frustrations.

It is so in the '60s. Two fears have come to dominate the thinking of our citizenry: the fear of mounting costs of public services that will somehow sap our economic fibre; and the fear of Russia's military, technological, and ideological threat to "bury" us. Across the country people have tended to "take out" these fears on our educational institutions.

On the one hand, principals and professors have been told they must step up the cadence of education if we are to compete with the quantity and quality of the big Red schoolhouse. On the other hand, presidents and superintendents have been warned they must shave close if we are to avoid oppressive taxation. Among the devices proposed by both practitioners and laymen to accomplish these ends is year-round education, a plan pictured as combining in happy fashion the efficiency of acceleration with economy of resources.

The call for academic calendar reform has provoked at least as much opposition as support. Proponents of the conventional pattern have questioned both the practicality of means and the validity of ends in year-round education. In the resulting debate, each side has tended to rely as much on emotional arguments as on reason and experience.

What are the facts?

THE PROS AND CONS

At the risk of over-simplifying both the reasons for and the facts against year-round education, let us reduce the claims and counter-claims to key points, and examine each in turn in the light of available data.

The Question of Economy

The lay support for year-round education stems to large degree from the proposition that the plan seems to encompass significant economies. In turn, professional opposition to year-round education bases arguments on the charge that such economies are more apparent than real.

Physical Plant. Theoretically, year-round education has the capability of reducing the need for added classrooms and related facilities in the face of mounting enrollment pressures.[1] If it takes 12 buildings to house "x" number of students attending two terms a year, it will take only 8 buildings to house the same number of students staggered over three terms a year. Or if it takes 12 buildings to house "x" number of students spending four years in school, it will take only 9 buildings to house the same number of students spending three years in school.

The mathematics are inescapable. Savings of from 25 to 33 per cent in physical plant construction are possible in theory under year-round education. But the human realities mitigating against the operation of the theory are equally inescapable. To achieve maximum economies, there must be total control of enrollment so as to achieve perfect balance among terms; otherwise you must still build to accommodate conventional autumn peaks.[2] Achieving such enrollment balance involves registration predictions and regulations for which neither administrators, students, nor parents have shown any stomach. And what of the public service and adult education activities that are wont to be conducted in academic buildings during the summer now? Would they not have to give way to undergraduate instruction?

The most one can say for physical plant economies inherent in year-round education is that, in the absence of regimented matriculation, such savings would be considerably less than the theoretical maximum, but they might nontheless be significant, particularly on an interim basis, depending on what any group of taxpayers deems significant. Even a 10 per cent reduction in building needs might be the difference between serving every able student and closing the doors of educational opportunity.

Faculty Salaries. The heaviest continuing cost of education is actually not in physical plant amortization but in personnel pay. Here, again, the proponents of year-round education see measurable economies. If it takes 120 instructors to teach "x" number of students attending two terms a year, it will take only 80 instructors to teach the same number of students staggered over three terms a year. Or if it takes 120 instructors to teach "x" number of students spending four years in school, it will take only 90 instructors to teach the same number of students spending three years in school.[3]

Again the mathematics are inescapable, but again so are the human realities. You cannot ask an instructor to teach three terms a year without paying him more than he receives for teaching two terms. If you pay him for summer instruction at full value, any physical-plant savings may be washed out, and then some. If you pay him at scab rates, you face a steady deterioration in the calibre of your faculty.

Whether you can even get instructors to teach year-round is another matter. At the high school level, it is likely that many would choose to trade summer vacations for 12-month salaries. But at the college and university level, where gifts and grants are increasingly available for research or travel, it is just as likely that few professors would volunteer to teach around the calendar. What is more, many administrations would feel constrained to insist that they not do so, in the interests of the institution's role in productive scholarship and public service. The net result would be that in order to maintain a year-round teaching operation you would have to increase your staff by some 33 per cent, with a third on leave in any given term. The budgetary implications are obvious. So are the recruiting problems.*

It is difficult to escape the conclusion that any economies gained in year-round education through niggardly treatment of staff will be achieved at the expense of educational quality. The problem is all the more serious in that the erosion may be delayed and subtle, but that it will show up in time is inevitable.

Parent-Student Expenses. How does the customer pocketbook fare under year-round education? The story is mixed. For many students, gainful summer employment is now the difference between family solvency and insolvency. On the other hand, the student who borrows in order to accelerate his education gains at least one full year of salary.

---

* The Research Division of the National Education Association reports that already educational institutions are having trouble recruiting sufficient qualified staff.

And it is not his salary the first year out of school that he gains; it is his last paycheck before retirement age. So it is theoretically possible under an all-year calendar to exchange $1,500 lost in summer wages for $15,000 in mature salary.[4]

For the student who elects not to accelerate but to stay out and work the terms of his choice, winter periods may offer more job opportunities in many urban areas; but in agricultural and recreational regions the summer period continues to offer the best short-term job market.[5]

In Summary. On balance, the all-year calendar may offer a temporary respite to building needs, but any savings in salary items will come directly out of the hides of instructors and indirectly out of the fabric of the institution. To the student willing to borrow against future income, the all-year calendar offers savings; to the student on a pay-as-you-go plan, it may or may not enhance his summer-time earning capacity.

In short, there is no budgetary magic in year-round education, and there can be serious pitfalls. Where capital investments are not keeping pace with the surge of students, however, the all-year calendar may be the only alternative to limiting enrollments or operating in jammed, second-rate facilities.

The Question of Acceleration

Professional support for year-round education stems to large degree from the proposition that the plan offers opportunities for curriculum acceleration and enrichment. We are told that in order to keep up with the Russian Joneses, we must turn out all manner of technicians and scientists at a much more rapid rate than we are now doing. We are told that the explosive accumulation of new knowledge in the post-war years demands an academic calendar with more latitude if we are to cram it all in without extending indefinitely the time spent in school. We are told that our youth spend too long a period in school now, anyway, and that they ought to start contributing to the economy at an earlier age since they will be retiring at an earlier age than was true even a generation ago.

Opponents of acceleration do not argue directly with these propositions, but they do claim that the penalties inherent in acceleration outweigh any gains.

Student Health and Maturity. That year-round education is somehow injurious to the physical and mental health of students is an argument of long standing. There is virtually no statistical evidence to support this claim and a good deal to counter it, as we have seen.[6] Yet the nagging fear persists, that without the conventional summer hiatus from his books the student will at worst burn out his brains or at least miss the bucolic joys of vacation revelries.

There is the corollary claim that students below standard age do not have the intellectual or social maturity to cope with academic life in all its aspects, much less with the life of a world into which they are thrust too early. Again there is no evidence to support this belief, and much that documents the opposite thesis.[7] Yet there remains the lurking reluctance to rob our youth of a leisurely academic pace. One series of studies may be definitive:

Pressey and Flesher made studies of the status as alumnae of large numbers of women who were graduated in an accelerated program. On the basis of such characteristics as entrance tests, grades, and courses of study these women were matched against controls who matriculated in a nonaccelerated or regular program.

Ten years after graduation, on the average, the "accelerates" as compared to the controls had obtained a significantly higher number of advanced degrees; and a significantly larger number of the accelerates were working after having been married. A slightly higher percentage of the nonaccelerates were married, and a slightly higher percentage of the accelerates had been divorced; but these differences were small. Both groups participated to about the same degree in community activities. These studies led Flesher and Pressey to conclude that many students of ability can complete a four-year program in less time with no unfortunate consequences.[8]

The Weather. That summertime learning is ineffective and even debilitating is an argument as old as summer sessions themselves. Some meteorological research tends to support this thesis, but academic data do not. Certainly in a day of air conditioning it is difficult to see why summer academic activity should be any less efficient than summer business activity.[9]

Faculty Ennui. Year-round work seems not to be depressing those elementary and high school teachers employed under such a system,[10] but college and university professors and administrators tend to be universally agreed that year-round teaching on anything like a continuous schedule is definitely undesirable.[11]

There are valid reasons for this seeming discrepancy. The school teacher has one principal responsibility: to teach. Given occasional sabbaticals, 11-month teaching need not be any more distressing than 11-month office work. The professor, on the other hand, has a triple responsibility: to teach, to do research, and to perform public services associated with his productive scholarship. He has traditionally used his so-called vacation period to accomplish these added functions, with or without extra reimbursement. To ask him to teach around the calendar robs him and his institution of time essential for essential duties.

While a college or university can itself adopt an all-year calendar, then, each individual professor cannot. This simply means that a campus staff must be large enough to permit a third of the instructors to be on leave in any given term.

Administrative Headaches. Year-round education admittedly introduces administrative problems.[12] It requires added stopping and starting of the academic procession. It discommodes intramural schedules and rules of eligibility. It will impose additional expense for certain housekeeping activities that are now carried on in the vacation periods. It may require revamping of fee schedules. Adult education programs may be pressed to find summer housing. Articulation with the schedules of sister institutions may be disrupted. There will be need for air-conditioned classrooms, laboratories, and offices. None of these problems seems insurmountable, although they may be irritating. As a bonus, most all-year calendars eliminate the "lame duck" period between Christmas vacation and the beginning of the winter term.

Looming largest of all, of course, is the problem of recruiting or regimenting enough students into each term to make the plan work. Until year-round education enters the socio-economic milieu, only enforcement or enticement will suffice, which leaves the administrator a choice between police tactics or Madison Avenue techniques.*

Public Needs. A major deterrent to the universal adoption of year-round education at the elementary and secondary level is the sanctity of the American family summer vacation. It will only be under duress that parents forgo this annual ceremony, yet they will have to rearrange their schedules drastically if their children are in a year-round school.[13]

A major deterrent to the year-round calendars at the university level is the need for offering short sessions for teachers. The conventional campus summer session was born as a service to teachers, and teachers continue to come in large numbers. They cannot come, of course, for longer than eight weeks or so. Consequently, unless a university elects to take itself out of the important business of up-grading elementary and high school teachers and administrators, it must continue to make provisions for their professional advancement. This means that either short summer sessions must be superimposed on the summer term—an expensive proposition—or that the summer term be split into increments short enough

* A recent survey by the Joint Office of Institutional Research, Washington, D.C., shows "no strong, consistent increase in numbers of freshmen entering state universities in June, immediately after high school graduation."

to accommodate school personnel. Either device complicates the emergence of the all-year calendar.

In Summary. On balance, the all-year calendar offers undeniable opportunities for acceleration, enrichment, or rehabilitation, and there is no substantial evidence to support the claim that year-round learning is deliterious to the student or the learning process. But getting teachers to teach and students to attend in summer, and getting the public to acquiesce —and pay the necessary bills—projects the whole question out of the realm of academic issues and into the very fabric of American life.

A RATIONALE

The academic calendar does not exist in a vacuum. On the one hand it is an educational instrument which has as its primary purpose to support the functions, policies, and goals of the institution it is designed to serve. On the other hand, it is a reflection of going patterns in public life. While its calendar is not the only educational instrument a school or college can adjust to meet changing needs or stimulate needed changes, the calendar is certainly one of the devices meriting continuous review as educational agencies seek to carry forward into a busy future their unique contributions to society.

The Need for Review

Are calendar innovations justified at this time? All but the most biased can recognize both some old and some new problems for which at least partial solutions may be found in calendar review:

1. The number of school- and college-age young people is growing explosively. To teach this greatly expanded student body will require the utmost use of every time and space resource at the country's command.

2. Present and prospective physical plants are often limited. In the years at hand, a serious building gap may exist.

3. With the mushrooming of new knowledge, the expansion of attendant curricula, and the continuing military service requirement, there is a need for a schedule that will permit students to compress the time required for completion of basic diploma and degree work. At the same time, there is need for a calendar that will permit students to intersperse attendance with jobs at optimum intervals.

4. As institutions of higher education expand their research and extension roles, optimum recruitment and utilization of staff requires a calendar of maximum flexibility.

5. The American pattern of life has changed, reflecting the emergence of an increasingly urban, industrial society. It is no longer necessary or even desirable, in many regions, to tie the academic calendar to the agricultural cycle.

6. If our educational institutions are to continue to win necessary public approval and support, they must constantly re-examine their internal systems of operation with the end in view of better meeting the social problems confronting the country.

7. Many present calendars have aggravating flaws which hopefully could be resolved under a revised schedule, particularly the "lame-duck" period following the Christmas recess, the roving nature of the spring recess, and the shortage of time for essential administrative chores between terms.

In short, the country faces a crisis in education. An unprecedented number of qualified young people are at the doors of our schools and colleges. This is in a sense a happy crisis, but it must be met with dispatch. America's traditional commitment is to universal education. It is inconceivable that we will bar the gates to adequate educational opportunity to any who have the ability to profit from learning.[14]

One of the educational devices which can be modified to help meet pressing new needs is the academic calendar. While such other devices as staggered, evening, and Saturday classes will help, they alone may not suffice. What looms as a necessity is a calendar with the ability to accommodate more students in a given time and space than does the conventional schedule, thus facilitating the extension of educational opportunities to millions of youth.

At the same time, calendar change must not mean the dilution of quality; indeed, it should provide a framework for improvement in educational functions. If educational enterprise is to meet the challenges of modern populations and modern times, it must also maintain the best of the academic standards that have developed over more than a century.

The Need for Criteria

In considering various calendars, it behooves professionals and public alike to pay close attention to a set of salient principles:

1. In essence the academic calendar should represent a framework for presenting effectively and efficiently throughout the year the educational programs with which the institution is charged. A calendar is not an end. It is a means to maintaining and enhancing the quality and quantity of performance. Viewed otherwise, calendar change can take a school or college down a spur track.

2. There is no one academic calendar that is best for all institutions. A sound calendar is indigenous, growing out of the particular traditions and needs of a particular institution and its constituency. Further, since no one calendar completely resolves all the associated problems, emphasis should be given to those systems which can be most effectively implemented, and most easily integrated with the present system, with the least amount of disruption to the educational program while accomplishing the most important objectives.

3. The calendar should provide a pattern by which students may profitably utilize the facilities and resources of the institution throughout the year as their own capabilities, finances, and objectives dictate. Flexible opportunities for teaching, study, and travel by the faculty should likewise be facilitated. Particularly, any new plan should meet the im-

portant needs of any student body which has traditionally enrolled for short periods only.

4. The calendar should be characterized by instructional periods of adequate length, by efficient breaks between instructional periods, by opportunities for educational service to groups other than full-time students, and by economical use of administrative time.

5. Unnecessary change should be avoided. No change should be recommended merely for the sake of a "new look." At the same time, practices of long standing should not blind us to needs for change.*

6. Above all, to pursue calendar changes as a sheer economy device is to pursue a mirage. By providing for increased utilization of existing physical facilities, a year-round calendar may postpone the need for new buildings, but only for a time. Without question there is implicit in any year-round calendar the fact that additional operating funds will be required. And if these operating funds are not allocated to the summer term on the same scale to which the fall and winter terms are accustomed, the year-round calendar becomes a vehicle for academic deterioration rather than for heightened service.[15]

Where Do We Go from Here?

As can be seen from an insightful examination of the criteria suggested above, the questions that need asking, the problems that need facing, and the prospects that need frank evaluation in any consideration of year-round education are by no means superficial. They go to the heart of the educational enterprise.

---

* A recent report to the Association of University Summer Session Deans and Directors (see *Preface*) lists these "appropriate reasons" for year-round operation: (1) When a significant part of an institution's potential student body desires acceleration, (2) when present summer curricula are inadequate, (3) enrollment pressures, (4) space shortages, (5) underemployment of faculty, and (6) desire to raise the quality of the summer program. The same report lists the following "vain" reasons for shifting to year-round instruction: (1) saving money, (2) better use of facilities, and (3) salary increases.

A school board, for example, cannot engage in sound calendar planning without first having clearly in mind the mission of its particular school. A college board must approach the academic calendar issue from the perspective of the particular needs of its student clientele. A university board that ignores profound faculty standards and mores in any calendar juggling does so at grave risk to the future of the institution.

Here, then, may lie the great utility of today's academic calendar debate. As professionals and laymen alike struggle with the question of an optimum schedule, they will perforce face the central issues in American education. They will renew their appreciation of an educational system which has become more and more an irreplaceable instrument of national policy, a vital tool for American survival. They will hone their understanding of the pivotal position of faculty-student relationships in the learning process. They will face again the unalterable fact that in education as in any enterprise money is the final factor that determines results. And they will experience fully that spirit of partnership that is the wonder and redemption of American public education: identifying public problems and public needs, focusing professional skills and resources on them, and translating learned insights into new educational programs that merit and win added public interest and support.[16]

What emerges from the current calendar controversy may or may not involve calendar changes, but if the great debate can be the occasion for fruitful internal analysis and heightened public understanding it will have served well the continuing evolution of American education for American society.

THE SITUATION TODAY

All levels of American education today are affected by the same forces: rising enrollments, limited funds for expansion, pressures for more education in less time. The provision of ever-expanding educational opportunities in the United States in the next 100 years is not impossible, but it is formidable. First, no one of us needs any documentation about the "baby boom." We can see it up the street, where a brand-new school already is crowded, and against the horizon, where the sun rises over roof on roof of homes sprouting in yesterday's cornfields. Second, the great surge of young people set to descend on our colleges and universities is not a statistical mirage, either. Almost every reliable estimate predicts that by 1970 the number seeking enrollment in institutions of higher learning will approach 7 million, by 1975 8,600,000. Third, the overwhelming evidence is that our society is becoming increasingly dependent on adults who have acquired a higher order of formal education and training. The demand for part-time professional and technical work can be expected to increase in the next 10 years at perhaps an even greater order of magnitude than the demand for undergraduate education. This crisis in education is rendered all the more urgent in an era of vastly accumulating knowledge, of explosive trends in technology, of sweeping urbanization, of continued international tension—pyramiding pressures that demand enlightened citizenship on a broad scale if the American way is to persist and flourish.

Providing classrooms and teachers for youngsters has already become the major enterprise for local municipalities. The number of youths who can afford a higher education will strain shortly the personnel and physical resources of existing campuses. For every student on a campus there could be an equally well-qualified youth who cannot afford to meet rising tuition rates or who cannot find room. At the same time, social and technological changes will bring increasingly to many adults—men and women—both the need to continue their education and some leisure in which to do so. These adult students will have to vie with vastly increased numbers of youth for educational opportunities in short supply.

The adults at our doors are not mere dabblers in education. Theirs is the need for rigorous refresher courses to qualify them for productive lives in an age of massive change. The youths seeking a college education now will live a part of their lives in the 21st century. The youngsters in our kindergartens deserve that access to learning that is the essence of the American dream. All three groups must be prepared to meet strenuous tests. Even the best models of education today may not be good enough or flexible enough. We have learned we are adaptable enough to defend ourselves, whatever the cost. We must now learn we are adaptable enough to educate ourselves as we need to be educated. Existing educational facilities and instructional personnel must be utilized to the utmost. We must reappraise present procedures and test new patterns, making changes where changes are indicated, yet removing none of those proverbial "ancient landmarks" which continue to be viable.

REFERENCES

Chapter 2

1 Rich, W. K. "Present Status of the All-Year Secondary School," *California Journal of Secondary Education*, January, 1956, p. 3.
2 Aker, Howard, *The All-Year School*, Milwaukee Superintendency Report, November, 1954, p. 2.
3 *Greater Utilization of School Building Facilities*, Wisconsin Legislative Council Report, May, 1958, p. 11.
4 *Ibid.*
5 *Ibid.*, p. 13.
6 *Year-Round School*, American Association of School Administrators Booklet, 1960, p. 4.
7 *Ibid.*
8 *Greater Utilization of School Building Facilities, op. cit.*, p. 21.
9 *Ibid.*, p. 17.
10 *The All-Year School Plan*, Report of the Joint Committee of Atlanta, DeKalb and Fulton County Schools, Georgia, May, 1957.
11 McCarty, Donald, "Is the All-Year School the Answer?", *Administrators Notebook*, February, 1958, p. 3.
12 *The All-Year School*, United States Office of Education Circular 470, 1958, p. 7.
13 *The All-Year School of Nashville, Tennessee*, Field Study Number 3, George Peabody College for Teachers, Nashville, Tenn., 1931, p. vii.
14 *Ibid.*
15 *The All-Year School, op. cit.*, p. 2.
16 Aker, "The All-Year School," *op. cit.*, p. 2.
17 *The All-Year School, op. cit.*, p. 3.
18 *Year-Round School, op. cit.*, p. 13.
19 *The Longer School Year*, Minnesota Department of Education Project 12, 1958, p. 10.
20 *Greater Utilization of School Building Facilities, op. cit.*
21 *The Longer School Year, op. cit.*
22 Milwaukee *Journal* editorial, December 10, 1929.
23 Milwaukee *Sentinel* editorial, March 15, 1930.
24 *Year-Round School Programs*, National Educational Association *Journal*, February, 1955, p. 82.
25 Miles, Dorothy, "Lexington's Year-Round School," *American School Board Journal*, March, 1952, p. 28.
55 *Ibid.*, p. 21.
56 *Ibid.*, p. 11.
57 *Ibid.*, p. 32.

26 Farrand, Wilson, and M. V. O'Shea, "The All-Year Schools in Newark," *School and Society*, April 10, 1926, p. 469.

27 *Ibid.*, p. 468.

28 Beveridge, J. H., "Omaha High Schools on All-Year Plan," *School Life*, October, 1925, p. 22.

29 *Ibid.*

30 Vanderslice, H. R., "Five Years' Experience with the All-Year School," *Elementary School Journal*, December, 1933, p. 257.

31 *Ibid.*

32 Vanderslice, H. R., "The All-Year School in Aliquippa, Pennsylvania," *Elementary School Journal*, April 10, 1930, p. 582.

33 Miles, Dorothy, "Lexington's Year-round School," *American School Board Journal*, March, 1952, p. 27.

34 *The All-Year School of Nashville, Tennessee*, Field Study Number 3, George Peabody College for Teachers, Nashville, Tenn., 1931, p. 50.

35 Brinkerhoff, G. I., "The Effects of All-Year Schools on Pupil Advancement," *Journal of Educational Method*, December, 1930, p. 169.

36 Brinkerhoff, G. I., "The Effects of All-Year Schools Upon Social Adjustment," *Journal of Educational Method*, February, 1931, p. 291.

37 *Ibid.*

38 Thompson, J., and L. Meyer, "What Research Says About Acceleration," *Journal of Secondary Education*, May, 1961, p. 302.

39 *Ibid.*, p. 304.

40 Brinkerhoff, G. I., "The Effects of All-Year Schools Upon Social Adjustment," *Journal of Educational Method*, February, 1931, p. 291.

41 *Ibid.*

42 *The All-Year School of Nashville, Tennessee*, *op. cit.* p. viii.

43 *Ibid.*, p. 26.

44 Brinkerhoff, "The Effects of All-Year Schools Upon Social Adjustment," *op. cit.*, p. 293.

45 *The All-Year School of Nashville, Tennessee*, *op. cit.*, p. 2.

46 Vanderslice, "Five Years' Experience with the All-Year School," *op. cit.*

47 *Ibid.*, p. 267.

48 Irons, H. S., "Utilizing Buildings and Instructional Materials 12 Months Annually," *American School Board Journal*, March, 1934, p. 19.

49 Brinkerhoff, "The Effects of All-Year Schools upon Pupil Advancement," *op. cit.*, p. 170.

50 *Ibid.*

51 *Ibid.*, p. 173.

52 Brinkerhoff, G. I., "The Effects of All-Year Schools upon Scholarship," *Journal of Educational Method*, January, 1931, p. 209.

53 *The All-Year School of Nashville, Tennessee*, *op. cit.* p. 10.

54 *Ibid.*, p. 14.

58 *Ibid.*, p. 33.
59 Huntingdon, Ellsworth, *Mainsprings of Civilization*, Wiley, New York, 1945, p. 348.
60 Brown, G. I., "The Relationship Between Barometric Pressure and Relative Humidity and Classroom Behavior," unpublished article, University of California, December 8, 1961, p. 6.
61 Dexter, E. G., "Conduct and the Weather," *The Psychological Review*, Vol. 2, 1899, p. 31.
62 Dexter, E. G., *Weather Influences*, Macmillan, New York, 1904, p. 107.
63 Farrand and O'Shea, "The All-Year Schools in Newark," *op. cit.*, p. 468.
64 *Greater Utilization of School Building Facilities, op. cit.*, p. 17.
65 *Year-Round School, op. cit.*, p. 7.
66 Irons, H. S., "Utilizing Buildings and Instructional Materials 12 Months Annually," *American School Board Journal*, March, 1934, p. 18.
67 Brinkerhoff, "The Effects of All-Year Schools upon Social Adjustment," *op. cit.*, p. 291.
68 Vanderslice, "The All-Year School in Aliquippa, Pennsylvania," *op. cit.*, p. 585.
69 Irons, "Utilizing Buildings and Instructional Materials 12 Months Annually," *op. cit.*, p. 19.
70 *Ibid.*
71 Tomancik, Mary, "All Year Schools," *The Nations Schools*, June, 1951, p. 69.
72 *Ibid.*, p. 70.
73 *Ibid.*, p. 71.
74 *Ibid.*
75 *Opinion Poll, The Nations Schools*, May, 1955, p. 6.
76 Farrand and O'Shea, "The All-Year Schools in Newark," *op. cit.*, p. 468.
77 *The All-Year School of Nashville, Tennessee, op. cit.*, p. 50.
78 *Ibid.*, p. 51.
79 Roe, Warren, "Comparative Costs of Integrated All-Year Schooling and of Part Time Schooling," *Journal of Educational Method*, March, 1931, p. 358.
80 *Greater Utilization of School Building Facilities, op. cit.*, p. 11.
81 Best, J. W., "A Year Round School Program," *School Executive*, October, 1953, p. 59.
82 *Ibid.*, p. 59.
83 *Ibid.*
84 Fitzpatrick, W. J., "The All-Year School, Pro and Con., *School and Society*, April 26, 1958, p. 191.
85 Grieder, C., "Let's Lengthen the School Year," *Nations Schools*, August, 1958, p. 28.
86 *Ibid.*

87 Crawford, Robert, "The Advantages and Disadvantages of the 12 Month School Year," *National Association of Secondary School Principals Bulletin,* April, 1958, p. 233.
88 Hartsell, H. C., "Twelve Month School," *National Association of Secondary School Principals Bulletin,* December, 1953, p. 23.
89 *Year-Round School, op. cit.,* p. 4.
90 *Ibid.*
91 Deacon, J. N., "Year Round Programs," *National Association of Secondary School Principals Bulletin,* April, 1956, p. 89.
92 MacPherson, J. D., "Keeping Schools Open All Year," *Nations Schools,* September, 1955, p. 52.
93 Clark, D. O., "Why Not an 11 Month School Year?", *School Executive,* March, 1958, p. 61.
94 *Ibid.*
95 Shaffer, Helen B., "Year-Round School, "*Editorial Research Reports,* Washington D. C., June 5, 1963, p. 419.
96 *Year-Round School,* op. cit., p. 13.
97 Shaffer, *op. cit.,* p. 422.
98 Williams, Robert F., "The Year-Round School Is Here," *Virginia Journal of Education,* December, 1962, p. 8.

Chapter 3

1 Tickton, Sidney G., *The Year-Round Campus Catches On,* The Fund for the Advancement of Education, New York, 1963, p. 6.
2 Hungate, Thad. L., and Earl J. McGrath, *A New Trimester Three-Year Program,* Bureau of Publications, Teachers College, Columbia University, New York, 1963.
3 Tickton, *op. cit.,* p. 6.
4 *Ibid.,* pp. 9 and 10.
5 *Ibid.,* pp. 7 and 8.
6 *The University Calendar,* American Association of Collegiate Registrars and Admissions Officers, 1961, p. 14.
7 Stecklein, Corcoran, and Ziebarth, *The Summer Session,* Bureau of Institutional Research Report Number 1, University of Minnesota, 1958, p. 3.
8 *A Statistical Portrait of the Wisconsin College Student,* Coordinating Committee for Higher Education in Wisconsin, Madison, December 31, 1961.
9 McKenna, David L., "The Academic Calendar in Transition," *Educational Record,* January, 1962, p. 70.
10 *Ibid.,* page 68.
11 *The University Calendar, op. cit.,* p. 9.
12 *Report on the University Calendar,* The University of Wisconsin History Department, Madison, 1960, p. 9.
13 *Ibid.*
14 *The University Calendar, op. cit.,* p. 8.
15 *Ibid.,* p. 9.
16 *Ibid,* p. 6.

17 *Michigan Report*, Commission on Year-Round Integrated Operation, University of Michigan, May 15, 1961, p. 32.
18 Easton, Elmer C., *Year-Round Operation of Colleges*, Engineering Research Bulletin 41, Rutgers State University, New Jersey, 1958, p. 33.
19 *The Longer School Year*, Supplement I, Joint Staff Study 31, Coordinating Committee for Higher Education, Wisconsin, January, 1960, p. 1.
20 *Ibid*, p. 2.
21 *Ibid*, p. 3.
22 Rankin, Alan C., "The Trimester Plan of the University of Pittsburgh," *Current Issues in Higher Education*, 1961, p. 167.
23 Eliot, C. W., *Educational Reform, Essays and Addresses*, Century, New York, 1905, p. 268.
24 Kirk, Grayson, "College Shouldn't Take Four Years," *Saturday Evening Post*, March 26, 1960, p. 21.
25 *Ibid.*, p. 108.
26 *Ibid*, p. 109.
27 *Ibid.*
28 *The University Calendar, op. cit.*, p. 26.
29 *Ibid.*, p. 27.
30 *The Longer School Year, op. cit.*, p. 21.
31 Hechinger, Fred, "A Cure for Growing Pains," *Saturday Review*, September 12, 1959, p. 20.
32 *Report of the Committee on the Trimester Calendar*, University of Pittsburgh Report, April 2, 1958.
33 *Summary of the "Trimester Meeting,"* University of Pittsburgh, June 15, 1960, p. 1.
34 *Ibid.*, p. 2.
35 Easton, *Year-Round Operation of Colleges, op. cit.*, p. 31.
36 *Ibid.*, p. 33.
37 *Ibid.*
38 *The Longer School Year, op. cit.*, p. 27.
39 *Ibid.*
40 *Ibid.*, p. 17.
41 *Ibid.*
42 *Ibid.*
43 *Ibid.*
44 *Ibid.*, p. 16.
45 *Report of the Committee on the Trimester Calendar*, University of Pittsburgh, April 2, 1958, p. 22.
46 *Proceedings of the Conference on the Trimester Calendar*, University of Pittsburgh, June 15, 1960, p.1, Part II.
47 *The Longer School Year, op. cit.*, p. 9.
48 *Michigan Report*, op. cit. p. 2.
49 *Ibid.*, p. 18.
50 Hungate and McGrath, *op. cit.*, p. 12–14.
51 *Ibid.*, pp. 30–31.
52 *Ibid.*, p. 37.

53 *Ibid.*, p. 40.
54 Eliot, *Educational Reform, op. cit.*, p. 151.
55 Lowell, A. L., *At War with Academic Traditions in America*, Harvard University Press, 1934, p. 255.
56 *Ibid.*
57 *Ibid.*, p. 256.
58 Pressey, S. L., *Educational Acceleration, Appraisals and Basic Problems*, Ohio State University, Educational Research Monograph 31, 1949, p. 6.
59 Farnsworth, D. L., *Mental Health in College and University*, Harvard University Press, 1957, p. 109.
60 Kirk, *op. cit.*, p. 111.
61 Cowley, W. H., "A Ninety Year Old Conflict Erupts Again," *Educational Record*, April, 1942, p. 195.
62 *Ibid.*, p. 208.
63 Pressey, *Educational Acceleration, op. cit.*, p. 25.
64 *Ibid.*
65 *Ibid.*, p. 26.
66 *Ibid.*, p. 25.
67 *Ibid.*, p. 29.
68 Pressey, *Educational Acceleration, op. cit.*, (Primary documents—U. S. Public Health Reports, 1940, Vol. LV, Part I, p. 58/Annals of Eugenics, II, pages 101–05/London Industrial Health Research Board, 1935), pp. 16–17.
69 *Ibid.*, p. 29.
70 *Ibid.*, (Primary documents—Jones, H. E., Conrad, H. S., "Growth and Decline of Intelligence," Genetic Psychology Monographs, XIII, March, 1953, pages 241–254/Miles, C. C. and Miles, W. R., "Correlation of Intelligence Scores and Chronological Age from Early to Late Maturity," *American Journal of Psychology*, XLIV, January, 1932, pages 51–70/Wechsler, D., *Measurement if Adult Intelligence*, Baltimore, Williams and Wilkins, 1939), pp. 28–30.
71 *Ibid.*, p. 31.
72 *Supplementary Information Relating to Year-Round School Proposals*, University of Wisconsin Institutional Study, October, 1959, p. 1.
73 Pressey, *Educational Acceleration, op. cit.*, p. 23.
74 *The Shape of Summer Sessions to Come*, Report of Seminar for University Administrators, edited by Clarence A. Schoenfeld, The University of Wisconsin, 1961, p. 23.
75 *Ibid.*, p. 24.
76 *Ibid.*, p. 57.
77 Wise, Max, "They Come for the Best of Reasons," American Council on Education, 1958, p. 21.
78 Pressey, *Educational Acceleration, op. cit.*, p. 22.
79 *Ibid.*, p. 98.
80 *Ibid.*, p. 102.
81 Tickton, *op. cit.*, p. 9.
82 *Ibid.*, p. 8.

83 *Ibid.*, p. 9.
84 *Ibid.*, p. 10.
85 Pressey, S. L., "Acceleration the Hard Way," *Journal of Educational Psychology*, April, 1944, p. 570.
86 *Report of the University Calendar Study Committee*, University of Michigan, June 19, 1958, p. 59.
87 "Columbia's Year-Round Medical Course," *School and Society*, January 4, 1958, p. 18.
88 *Ibid.*
89 Silverman, Y., and Vernon, "A Study of Early Entrance to College," *Journal of Educational Psychology*, 1932, Vol. 32, p. 71.
90 Sarabaugh, M. E., "The Younger College Student," *School and Society*, 1938, Vol. 40, p. 824.
91 Flesher, Maria, "An Intensive Study of Sixty-Seven Women who Obtained Their Undergraduate Degrees in Three Years or Less," *Journal of Educational Research*, 1946, Vol. 39, p. 606.
92 *Ibid*, p. 609.
93 Flesher, Marie, "Did They Graduate Too Young?", *Educational Research Bulletin*, 1949, p. 221.
94 *School and Society*, September 22, 1962, p. 299.
95 Chapman, G. O., "The Effects of Acceleration on Social and Academic Achievement," *Journal of Higher Education*, March, 1960, p. 144.
96 *Ibid.*
97 *Ibid.*, p. 148.
98 Robinson, F. P., "The Effect of Year-Round Attendance on Students," *Journal of Higher Education*, November 1943, p. 441.
99 *Ibid.*, p. 442.
100 *Ibid.*
101 *Ibid.*, p. 443.
102 *Ibid.*
103 *Report of the University Calendar Committee*, University of Michigan, *op. cit.*, p. 27.
104 *Use of Time During 1961 Summer by Students Registered During 1961 Fall Semester*, University of Wisconsin Institutional Study, May, 1962, p. 74.
105 *Ibid.*
106 *Progress Report on Year-Round Education*, University of Pittsburgh, 1960, p. 4.
107 *Progress Report on Year-Round Education*, University of Pittsburgh, 1961, p. 4.
108 *Michigan Report*, Year-Round Integrated Operation, *op. cit.*, p. 13.
109 Huntingdon, Ellsworth, *Mainsprings of Civilization*, Wiley, New York, 1945, p. 348.
110 Kanun, Ziebarth, and Abrahams, *Comparison of Student Achievement in the Summer Term and Regular Quarter—A Pilot Study*, University of Minnesota, August, 1961, p. 15.
111 *Ibid*, p. 35.
112 *Ibid.*

113 *Ibid.*
114 Angiolillo, P. F., *Armed Forces Foreign Language Teaching*, S. F. Vanni, 1947, pages 30 and 279.
115 *Ibid.*, p. 39.
116 Rehder and Twaddell, "ASTP at Wisconsin," *German Quarterly*, November, 1944, p. 221.
117 Adams, Walter, "Can Our Schools Teach the GI Way?", *Reader's Digest*, February, 1944, p. 47.
118 *The Longer School Year, op. cit.*, p. 17.
119 *Report of the University Calendar Study Committee*, University of Michigan, *op. cit.*, p. 59.
120 *Proceedings of the Conference on Year-Round Education*, University of Pittsburgh, March 9, 1961, p. 1.
121 *Ibid.*, p. 3.
122 *Conference on the Trimester Calendar*, University of Pittsburgh, June 15, 1960, p. 8.
123 *Conference on Year-Round Education*, University of Pittsburgh, *op. cit.*
124 *Ibid.*, p. 3.
125 *Ibid.*
126 *Conference on the Trimester Calendar*, University of Pittsburgh, *op. cit.*, p. 6.
127 *Conference on Year-Round Education*, University of Pittsburgh, *op. cit.*
128 Caplow, Theodore and Reece J. McGee, *The Academic Marketplace*, Basic Books, New York, 1958, p. 82.
129 Tickton, *op. cit.*, p. 9.
130 McKenna, "The Academic Calendar in Transition," *Educational Record*, 1962, Vol. 43, p. 69.
131 *Conference on the Trimester Calendar*, University of Pittsburgh, *op. cit.*, p. 9.
132 *Michigan Report*, Year-Round Integrated Operation, *op. cit.*, p. 4.
133 McKenna, "The Academic Calendar in Transition", *op. cit.*, p. 74.
134 Easton, *Year-round Operation of Colleges, op. cit.*, p. 33.
135 *Ibid.*
136 *The Longer School Year, op. cit.*, p. 27.
137 *Proceedings of the Trimester Conference*, University of Pittsburgh, *op. cit.*, p. 6.
138 *Report of the University Calendar Study Committee*, University of Michigan, *op. cit.*, p. 59.
139 *Michigan Report*, Year-Round Integrated Operation, *op. cit.*, p. 62.
140 *Proceedings of the Trimester Conference*, University of Pittsburgh, *op. cit.*, p. 1.
141 Hungate and McGrath, *op. cit.*, p. 26.
142 *Conference on the Trimester Calendar*, University of Pittsburgh, *op. cit.*, p. 4.
143 Roe, Warren, "Comparative Costs of Integrated All-Year Schooling and of Part-time Schooling," *Journal of Educational Method*, March, 1931, p. 358.

144 *Proceedings of the Trimester Conference,* University of Pittsburgh, *op. cit.*
145 McGrath, Earl J., "Plea for the Year-Round College," *New York Times Magazine,* April 28, 1963, p. 69.
146 The University of Illinois, *Faculty Letter,* February 7, 1963, p. 2.
147 Editorial Research Reports, *News Brief,* June 5, 1963, p. 2.
148 Ziebarth, E. W., "The Summer Session: A Research View," unpublished paper presented at North Central Conference on Summer Schools, Chicago, March 18, 1963.
149 Marsh, Gerald E., unpublished remarks at Association of University Summer Sessions Deans and Directors, Washington, D. C., October 7, 1963.

Chapter 4

1 *Greater Utilization of School Building Facilities,* Wisconsin Legislative Council Report, May, 1958, p. 21.
2 Easton, Elmer C., "Year-Round Operation of Colleges," *Engineering Research Bulletin 41,* Rutgers, The State University, New Jersey, 1958, p. 53.
3 *Greater Utilization of School Building Facilities, op. cit.,* p. 17.
4 *Use of Time During 1961 Summer by Students Registered during 1961 Fall Semester,* University of Wisconsin Institutional Study, May, 1962, p. 74.
5 *Michigan Report,* "Year-Round Integrated Operation," 1961, p. 13.
6 Vanderslice, H. R., "Five Years' Experience with the All-Year School," *Elementary School Journal,* December, 1933, p. 257.
7 Flesher, Marie, "An Intensive Study of Sixty-Seven Women Who Obtained Their Undergraduate Degrees in Three Years or Less," *Journal of Educational Research,* 1946, Vol. 39, p. 606.
8 Freedman, Mervin B., "Studies of College Alumni," in *The American College,* John Wiley & Sons, New York, 1962, p. 866.
9 Huntingdon, Ellsworth, *Mainsprings of Civilization,* Wiley, New York, 1945, p. 348.
10 Vanderslice, "The All-Year School in Aliquippa, Pennsylvania," *Elementary School Journal,* April, 1930, p. 585.
11 *Supplementary Information Relating to Year-Round School Proposals,* University of Wisconsin Institutional Study, October, 1959, p. 1.
12 Tomancik, Mary, "All Year Schools," *The Nations Schools,* June, 1951, p. 69.
13 Vanderslice, "The All-Year School in Aliquippa, Pennsylvania," *op. cit.,* p. 582.
14 McKenna, David L., "The Academic Calendar in Transition," *Educational Record,* January, 1962, p. 70.
15 *Michigan Report,* "Year-Round Integrated Operation," 1961, p. 2.
16 Schoenfeld, Clarence A., *The University and Its Publics,* Harper, New York, 1954, p. 171.